Building Modular Cloud Apps
with OSGi

Paul Bakker and Bert Ertman

O'REILLY®

Beijing · Cambridge · Farnham · Köln · Sebastopol · Tokyo

Building Modular Cloud Apps with OSGi

by Paul Bakker and Bert Ertman

Copyright © 2013 Paul Bakker and Bert Ertman. All rights reserved.

Printed in the United States of America.

Published by O'Reilly Media, Inc., 1005 Gravenstein Highway North, Sebastopol, CA 95472.

O'Reilly books may be purchased for educational, business, or sales promotional use. Online editions are also available for most titles (*http://my.safaribooksonline.com*). For more information, contact our corporate/institutional sales department: 800-998-9938 or *corporate@oreilly.com*.

Editor: Meghan Blanchette	**Indexer:** BIM Indexing and Proofreading Services
Production Editor: Rachel Steely	**Cover Designer:** Randy Comer
Copyeditor: Amanda Kersey	**Interior Designer:** David Futato
Proofreader: Linley Dolby	**Illustrator:** Rebecca Demarest

September 2013:   First Edition

Revision History for the First Edition:

2013-09-05:   First release

See *http://oreilly.com/catalog/errata.csp?isbn=9781449345150* for release details.

ISBN: 978-1-449-34515-0

[LSI]

To Qiushi, my love, for supporting all my crazy ideas and always being there for me.

— Paul Bakker

To Jorien, my incredible wife, and to Amber, my beautiful and joyful daughter. Thank you girls for supporting me throughout my career and for putting up with me. I love you!

— Bert Ertman

Table of Contents

Preface

The increasing complexity of software systems, together with the agile way in which we develop and evolve them today, demand an approach that makes the architecture of such systems deal with change. The solution to this challenge is called *modularity*. Modularity is a core design principle that makes code easier to understand and maintain by splitting it into small, isolated modules. This is not a new concept, but becomes more relevant each day. A modular code base lets us change, refactor, or simply replace code of modules without breaking other parts of the system. This makes modularity the ultimate agile tool.

Bringing modularity from the design to the runtime is not always easy and straightforward and cannot be done with plain Java alone. The only mature modularity solution for Java is OSGi. Over the years, OSGi has had the reputation of being too complex and difficult to use. Recently a lot has changed in the area of tooling and frameworks, however, bringing it on par with the development experience of traditional development stacks. With this we can focus on writing code while keeping an architectural focus on modularity.

This book describes how to apply those tools and techniques available today, and gives pragmatic insights into getting up and running with the required technology in no time. Using easy to understand, concise, but real-world code samples, we explore the application of modularity toward a new breed of web applications; software as a service over the Internet, more affectionately known as *cloud applications*. Along the way, we address typical cloud-age topics such as RESTful Web Services, NoSQL, Provisioning, Elasticity, Auto-Scaling, Hot Updates, and Automated Failover.

Who Should Read This Book

Primarily, this book is targeted to experienced enterprise Java developers who have a keen interest in modularity and who are looking for solutions to overcome some of today's most advanced software development problems: how to deal with change and how to manage complexity in a code base. The authors of this book use the tools and techniques described throughout the book in everyday development and have put some sophisticated cloud applications in production using them. A significant part of what you will learn here is based upon OSGi. We will focus on practical advice, rather than the more theoretical approach commonly found in other books and resources.

The book will also be useful to developers who have tried using OSGi in the past, but for some reason got stuck. Because OSGi is not a product owned by a single vendor, it is sometimes hard to find hands-on, to-the-point information on how to get things working. To those readers, this book can be an approachable and practical guide to become unstuck and get things going again. By no means is this book a complete OSGi reference, but it does contain everything that you need to know in order to build sophisticated applications in the cloud age.

How This Book Is Organized

This book is organized into three parts. Part I introduces the concepts of modularity from a high-level perspective and translates these to actual implementation details. Part II focuses on developing cloud applications and the tools and technologies required. Part III deals with deploying these applications to production and setting up advanced cloud infrastructure capabilities such as auto-scaling and failover.

Additionally, Appendix A describes an example application that puts everything from this book together in a showcase. The code of this application is hosted online, and the appendix contains instructions on how to get it.

Conventions Used in This Book

The following typographical conventions are used in this book:

Italic
> Indicates new terms, URLs, email addresses, filenames, and file extensions.

`Constant width`
> Used for program listings, as well as within paragraphs to refer to program elements such as variable or function names, databases, data types, environment variables, statements, and keywords.

`Constant width bold`
> Shows commands or other text that should be typed literally by the user.

`Constant width italic`
> Shows text that should be replaced with user-supplied values or by values determined by context.

This icon signifies a tip, suggestion, or general note.

 This icon indicates a warning or caution.

Using Code Examples

This book is here to help you get your job done. In general, if example code is offered with this book, you may use it in your programs and documentation. You do not need to contact us for permission unless you're reproducing a significant portion of the code. For example, writing a program that uses several chunks of code from this book does not require permission. Selling or distributing a CD-ROM of examples from O'Reilly books does require permission. Answering a question by citing this book and quoting example code does not require permission. Incorporating a significant amount of example code from this book into your product's documentation does require permission.

We appreciate, but do not require, attribution. An attribution usually includes the title, author, publisher, and ISBN. For example: "*Building Modular Cloud Apps with OSGi* by Paul Bakker and Bert Ertman (O'Reilly). Copyright 2013 Paul Bakker and Bert Ertman, 978-1-449-34515-0."

You can download the full source code from GitHub (*http://bit.ly/14DTna9*). For more detailed instructions on downloading the code, please see the section "Finding and Running the Source Code" on page 173.

If you feel your use of code examples falls outside fair use or the permission given above, feel free to contact us at *permissions@oreilly.com*.

Safari® Books Online

 Safari Books Online is an on-demand digital library that delivers expert content in both book and video form from the world's leading authors in technology and business.

Technology professionals, software developers, web designers, and business and creative professionals use Safari Books Online as their primary resource for research, problem solving, learning, and certification training.

Safari Books Online offers a range of product mixes and pricing programs for organizations, government agencies, and individuals. Subscribers have access to thousands of books, training videos, and prepublication manuscripts in one fully searchable database from publishers like O'Reilly Media, Prentice Hall Professional, Addison-Wesley Professional, Microsoft Press, Sams, Que, Peachpit Press, Focal Press, Cisco Press, John Wiley & Sons, Syngress, Morgan Kaufmann, IBM Redbooks, Packt, Adobe Press, FT Press, Apress, Manning, New Riders, McGraw-Hill, Jones & Bartlett, Course Technology, and dozens more. For more information about Safari Books Online, please visit us online.

How to Contact Us

Please address comments and questions concerning this book to the publisher:

O'Reilly Media, Inc.
1005 Gravenstein Highway North
Sebastopol, CA 95472
800-998-9938 (in the United States or Canada)
707-829-0515 (international or local)
707-829-0104 (fax)

We have a web page for this book, where we list errata, examples, and any additional information. You can access this page at *http://oreil.ly/Build_Cloud_Apps*.

To comment or ask technical questions about this book, send email to *bookques tions@oreilly.com*.

For more information about our books, courses, conferences, and news, see our website at *http://www.oreilly.com*.

Find us on Facebook: *http://facebook.com/oreilly*

Follow us on Twitter: *http://twitter.com/oreillymedia*

Watch us on YouTube: *http://www.youtube.com/oreillymedia*

Acknowledgments

A number of individuals share the credit for this book's development and delivery. First and foremost, many thanks to O'Reilly for trusting in us and providing us the opportunity to write this book. The team provided excellent support throughout the editing, reviewing, proofreading, and publishing process.

The authors would like to express their gratitude to the many people who helped or provided support in this journey. In particular, we would like to thank Meghan Blanchette, our editor, who provided us with excellent editorial help throughout all the stages of writing, helping with interim reviews, providing feedback on content and styling, and connecting us to the rest of team at O'Reilly.

The detailed proofreading by Marcel Offermans and Arun Gupta ensured that the material was technically accurate and true to the topics of the book. Their vast experience and knowledge showed in the depth of their comments.

Finally, we would like to thank Luminis, our employer, for its encouragement and for providing us with trust and resources to combine writing this book with our daily jobs.

PART I

Introducing Modularity in Java

CHAPTER 1
Modularity Introduction

Dealing with change is one of the most fundamental issues in building applications. It doesn't have to be difficult, however, since we are dealing with software that is not constrained to any physical laws. Change is an architectural issue, but unfortunately, it is often overlooked as such. This is logical to some extent, because most of the time you simply cannot see it coming.

Traditional software development processes can make it hard to cope with change. In waterfall, and even DSDM and RUP to some extent, the big design is being done up front. Once the design is created, it is carved in stone, and further down the line, there is rarely any possibility to divert from the original ideas. As soon as the first big chunks of functionality are built, it is pretty much impossible to get a fundamental change in the software design.

When using an agile methodology, you must have all disciplines involved: requirements, architecture, development, testing, and so on. As most activities of the software development process are performed in short iterations (or sprints), this affects the way that one activity can influence the remainder of the development process. Shorter development cycles can lead to a greater transparency. But they can also keep you from seeing the entire effect of certain architectural decisions when you first encounter them. Some parts of an application's architecture are harder to change than others. The key thing when dealing with change is to predict where it is coming, and delay any permanent architectural decisions until you have all necessary information for those decisions. This is hard, of course. On the other hand, a completely flexible application architecture is also impossible to achieve. Flexibility will likely cause so many abstractions that the complexity of the resulting application is unreasonably high. Complexity is a monster and should be avoided at all cost. It was Leonardo da Vinci who said, "Simplicity is the ultimate sophistication," and he is absolutely right about that.

Dealing with Increasing Complexity

A number of studies have been conducted that show how the number of lines of code double about every seven years. Not only are we building bigger applications, but we are also using more diverse technologies. Advanced mechanisms such as Aspect Oriented Programming, Polyglot Programming (using multiple programming languages within the same solution), the enormous amount and availability and diversity of open source frameworks for all layers of the application, using alternative storage solutions in the form of NoSQL, the need for multitenancy in PaaS and SaaS environments, dealing with massive scale and elastic resource allocation, etc, etc. Currently, complexity is rising at such a disturbing pace that we have to put mechanisms in place to bring it to a halt.

More complexity usually means spending more time understanding what the application actually does. Not to mention the amount of time, energy, and money that has to be invested in maintaining these applications for a long time. As an example, how many times have you looked at some code that you had written yourself a couple of years ago and had a hard time understanding what it actually does? With the evolution in which open source frameworks are being made available into the market, the amount of knowledge to keep up with in your teams is also very hard to deal with. This is also why writing readable code is so important. Rather name your variable `l` instead of `listOf Books`? You save some typing now but will regret it later on.

Divide and Conquer

Why is it difficult to maintain a large code base over many years? Many projects get into more and more problems as soon as the code base becomes larger. The core of the problem is that the code is not modular: there is no clear separation between different parts of the code base. Because of that, it becomes difficult to understand what the code is doing. To understand a nonmodular code base, you basically need to understand all the code, which is unrealistic. Working on a large code base that you can only partly comprehend will introduce bugs in places you couldn't foresee whenever you make any changes. We have all seen these kind of projects, and we all know what is wrong with them; they ended up as spaghetti code.

This can be improved by identifying separate parts of a system and strictly separating them from other parts of the code. Doing so starts with one of the most basic object orientation best practices: *program to interfaces, not to implementations*. By programming to interfaces only, you can make changes to implementations without breaking consumers of the interface. We all know and apply this every day, but code bases still end up as an unmaintainable mess. In real applications, we are dealing with several interfaces and implementation classes when working on a part of a system. How do you know which interfaces and classes belong together and should be seen as one piece when looking at the bigger picture? By programming to interfaces, we try to prevent coupling. At the same time, there is always some coupling, between classes. Without any coupling there wouldn't be any useful code. Again, we are looking at a basic object orientation best practice: *promote cohesion; prevent coupling.* In fact, this best practice can be seen as the golden rule of modular software design. Code that logically belongs together should be cohesive; it should do only one thing. The goal is to prevent coupling between these logical cohesive parts.

How can we communicate and enforce cohesion in separated *parts* of the code base while keeping coupling between them low? This is a far more difficult question. Object orientation and design patterns do give us the tools to deal with this at the finest level of single classes and interfaces. It doesn't give much guidance in dealing with groups of classes and interfaces. The Java language itself doesn't have any tools for this. We need something at a higher level: techniques to deal with well-defined groups of classes and interface, i.e., logical parts of a system. Let's call them *modules.*

Modularizing a software design refers to a logical partitioning of the system design that allows complex software to be manageable for the purpose of implementation and maintenance. The logic of partitioning may be based on related functions, implementation considerations, data, or other criteria. The term *modularity* is widely used, and systems are deemed *modular* when they can be decomposed into a number of components that may be mixed and matched in a variety of configurations. Such components are able to connect, interact, or exchange resources (data) in some way by adhering to a standardized interface. Modular applications are systems of components that are *loosely coupled.*

Service Oriented Architecture All Over Again?

If you have ever heard of Service Oriented Architecture (SOA), you might recognize that it proposes a solution to the problems discussed. The SOA promise is in fact even better (on paper). With SOA, we reuse existing systems, creating flexible and reusable business process services to an extent that new business requirements can be implemented by simply mixing and matching services. Theoretically speaking. Many of the SOA promises were never delivered and probably never will be because integrating systems at this level has many challenges. There is something very valuable in the concept, however. Isolating reusable parts of a larger system makes a lot of sense.

SOA is not the solution for the problems discussed in this book. SOA is on a very different architectural level: the level of integrating and reusing systems. Modularity is about implementing systems and about separating concerns within such a system. Modularity is about writing code; SOA is about system integration. Some have tried to apply patterns from the SOA world within a single system because it does theoretically solve the spaghetti code problem. You could identify parts of an application and implement them as separate "services." This is basically what we are looking for, but the patterns that are related to SOA are not fit for use within a single system. Applying integration patterns introduces a lot of complexity and overhead, both during development and runtime. It's an extreme form of over-engineering and dramatically slows down development and maintenance. Instead, we need something to apply the same concepts in a way that makes sense on the scale of classes and interfaces, with minimal development and runtime overhead.

A Better Look at Modularity and What It Really Means

Understanding the golden rule of software design and designing a system on paper such that it promotes cohesion between separate parts of the application and minimizes coupling between them is not the hardest part of applying modularity to software design. To create a truly modular system, it is important to not only have it modular in the design phase, but to also take that design and implement it in such a way that it is still modular at runtime. Modularity can therefore be subdivided in both *design time modularity* and *runtime modularity*. In the next few paragraphs, we are going to explore them a bit.

Design Time Modularity

Modularity is an architectural principle that starts at design time. Modules and relationships between modules have to be carefully identified. Similar to object-oriented programming, there is no silver bullet that will magically introduce modularity. There are trade-offs to be made, and patterns exist to help you do so. We will show many examples of this throughout the book. The most important step toward modularity is coming up with a logical separation of modules. This is basically what most architects will do, but they do this on the level of systems and layers. We need to do this on the code level as well, on a much more fine-grained level. This means that modularity doesn't come for free: we need to actively work toward it. Just throwing a framework in the mix will not make a system modular all of a sudden.

Runtime Modularity

Design time modularity can be applied to any code base, even if you are on a traditional nonmodular Java EE application server. Identifying modules in a design will already help, creating a clear design. Without a runtime environment that respects modules, it is very hard to enforce modularity. *Enforcing* sounds like a bad thing, and you might say that it is the role of developers to respect modularity. It certainly is our job as developers to do so, but we can use some help. It is very difficult to not accidentally break modularity by just relying on standards and guidelines when working in a large code base. The module borders are simply too vague to spot mistakes. Over time, small errors will leak into the code base, and finally modularity will just slowly evaporate.

It's much easier to work with modules if our runtime supports it. The runtime should at least:

- Enforce module isolation
- Enforce and clarify module dependencies
- Provide a services framework to consume modules

Enforcing module isolation is making sure that other modules are not using internal classes. A module should only be used by an explicitly defined API, and the runtime should make sure that other classes and interfaces are not visible to the outside world (other modules). Enforcing module dependencies is making sure that modules only depend on a well defined set of other modules, and a module should not load when its dependencies are not resolved to prevent runtime errors. Services are another key aspect of modularity, and we will talk a lot more about them in the next chapter.

Modularity Solutions

In essence, one could say that classes are a pretty modular concept. However, they are very limited in a way that you cannot have much structure materialized in just plain classes. Grouping classes can be done using the concept of packages, but the intention of packages is more to provide a mechanism to organize classes in namespaces belonging to a similar category or providing similar functionality. Within a package, it is not possible to hide certain classes from classes in other packages or even from classes in the same package. Sure there are some tricks, such as inner classes, or classes contained in other classes, but in the end this does not give you a truly modular concept.

An important aspect of runtime modularity is the packaging of the deployment artifact. On the Java platform, the JAR file has been the traditional unit of deployment. A JAR file holds a collection of classes or packages of classes, and their resources, and has the ability to carry some metadata about that distribution. Unfortunately, the Java runtime treats all JAR files as equal, and the information in the metadata description is ignored by both the classloader and the virtual machine. In plain Java and Java EE, all classes found in deployed JAR files are put in one large space, the classpath. In order to get the concept of runtime modularity to work, an additional mechanism is needed.

The basic idea of working on a modular approach using JAR files is not a bad one at all. JAR files are not only a unit of deployment, but also a unit of distribution, a unit of reuse, and a unit that you can add a version to.

There have been a number of attempts of enabling Java with a modular runtime. OSGi was an early candidate, given its Java Specification Request (JSR 8) number, but mostly because of political reasons and colliding characters, this never had a chance of success. Halfway through the 2000s, the concept of the Java Module System (JSR 277) was introduced, but it never made it into the Java runtime. As part of the original plans for

Java SE 7, in what was later to become the final days of Sun as the steward of Java, a new plan for modularity was launched under its codename *Jigsaw*. Then there is Maven, which was originally designed to be a building system isolating application modules and managing dependencies. Finally, vendors such as RedHat have attempted to create a modularity system. In the next paragraphs, we will take a better look at the solutions that are available in Java today.

OSGi

OSGi is the best known modularity solution for Java. Unfortunately, it also has a reputation for being an over-engineered, hard-to-use technology. To start with the latter: it's not. Many of the complaints are due to misunderstanding and inadequate tooling. It is true that OSGi is a complex specification. OSGi has been in use for over 10 years, in many different kind of systems. Because of this, there are many corner cases that the specification should facilitate. This is not over-engineering, but the result of evolving a standard for many years. The good news is that you won't have to deal with most of the complexity as an application developer or architect. Understanding the basics and, more important, understanding basic modularity patterns will get you a long way. That, combined with the greatly improved tooling available today, makes OSGi hardly any more difficult to use than Java without OSGi. And it gives you the power of modularity and some really nice development features as a side effect. The rest of the book will use OSGi as the technology to work with, and instead of trying to convince you that OSGi is easy to work with, we will get you started as soon as possible and let you see for yourself.

Jigsaw

The most interesting alternative for OSGi seems to be Jigsaw, as it is supposed to become the standard Java modularity solution. There is one problem however: it doesn't exist yet and will not anytime soon. Jigsaw was delayed for Java SE 8 and then again deferred to Java SE 9, which is currently scheduled for 2015–2016. The current scope of Jigsaw is also far from sufficient to build truly modular applications. It will merely be the basis to modularize the JDK itself and a basis for future work, post Java 9. Jigsaw is trying to solve two problems at the same time: modularizing the JDK itself and pushing the same model to developers. Splitting the JDK into smaller pieces makes a lot of sense, especially on "small" devices. Because of all the legacy, this is a much more difficult challenge than creating modular applications. To facilitate the JDK modularization, there will be some new language constructs to define modules, and this will also be available to developers. Unfortunately the proposal is based on concepts that will not be sufficient for application modularization. If you are looking at modularity today, Jigsaw is simply not a viable alternative. Will Jigsaw eventually be an OSGi killer? That is for the future to tell.

JBoss Modules

JBoss Modules is the modularity solution developed by RedHat as the basis of JBoss Application Server 7. JBoss Modules was developed with one very specific goal: startup speed of the application server. Because of this goal, JBoss Modules does a lot less than OSGi to make it faster at startup time. This made JBoss AS7 one of the fastest application servers to start up, but JBoss Modules an inadequate modularity solution for general use. The most important concept that JBoss Modules lacks is a dynamic service layer, which is the most important modularity concept while building applications. So far, there has also been little effort on making JBoss Modules usable outside of JBoss; documentation and real-life examples are very limited.

Maven

Although Maven isn't really a modularity solution, it is often discussed in this context. By separating a code base in smaller projects and splitting APIs and implementations in separate Maven projects, you can get pretty decent compile time modularity. As discussed previously, compile time modularity is only half of the solution. We need runtime modularity as well, and Maven doesn't facilitate in this at all. However, you could very well use Maven for compile time modularity while using OSGi for runtime modularity. This has been done in many projects and works well. In this book, you will see that you do not need Maven at all when using OSGi. OSGi modules (bundles) already contain the metadata required to define modules, and we don't need to duplicate this in our build environment. Maven itself is slow and painful to use, and it's difficult to get very fast turnarounds on code changes. For those reasons, and the fact that we actually don't need Maven at all, we don't advise using it as a modularity solution.

Choosing a Solution: OSGi

OSGi is the only mature modularity solution for Java today, and that is unlikely to change anytime soon. Although OSGi has been criticized for being too complex to use in the past, recent improvements to tooling and frameworks have changed this completely. The remainder of this book will be focused on using OSGi to achieve modularity. Although the concepts discussed in this book would work with any modularity framework, we want to keep the book as practical as possible for solving today's problems.

What Is OSGi?

OSGi is a modularity framework for the Java platform. The OSGi Alliance started work on this in 1999 to support Java on devices such as set-top boxes, service gateways, and all kinds of consumer electronics. Nowadays OSGi is applied in a much broader field and has become the de facto modularity solution in Java.

The OSGi framework is specified in the OSGi Core Specification, which describes the inner workings of the OSGi framework. Next to the OSGi Core Specification there is the OSGi Compendium Specification, which describes a set of standardized OSGi services such as the Log Service, Configuration Admin, and the HTTP Service. Several of the compendium services will be used in this book. Additionally, there is Enterprise OSGi, a set of specifications focused on using OSGi in an enterprise environment. This includes Remote Services, the JDBC Service, and the JPA Service. Besides these specifications, there are a number of lesser-known compendiums for residential and mobile usage that are not covered in this book.

When using OSGi, you need an implementation. The most popular OSGi implementations are Apache Felix and Equinox from the Eclipse Foundation. Both are mature implementations, but the authors of this book do have a preference for Apache Felix, because Equinox tends to be a little more heavyweight, and there are some implementation choices that only make sense for Eclipse usage. Therefore, Apache Felix is the implementation of our choice used throughout this book. It really doesn't matter much which implementation is used however, because the bundles you create and the compendium services run on any implementation.

You should understand that an OSGi framework such as Apache Felix only offers an implementation of the OSGi Core Specification. When you want to use the compendium or enterprise services, you will need implementations for those as well. The great thing about this is that you never bloat your runtime with anything that you are not using. Compare that to traditional application servers.

OSGi in the Real World

OSGi has a very long tradition of being used in all kinds of different systems. Its history started in embedded systems such as cars and home automation gateways, where modularity was mostly envisioned as a way for modules from different vendors to coexist in the same framework, giving them independent lifecycles so they could be added and updated without having to constantly reboot the system. Another well known example is the Eclipse IDE. Eclipse is built entirely on top of OSGi, which enables the Eclipse plug-in system. While Eclipse is probably the best known OSGi example, you can consider it the worst example as well. There are many Eclipse-specific design decisions that were necessary to support the Eclipse ecosystem but can be considered bad practices for most other applications.

In more recent years, we have seen a move toward the *enterprise* world of software, starting with application servers that based their core inner constructs on OSGi, such as Oracle GlassFish Application Server and IBM WebSphere® Application Server. The main reasons for this move to OSGi was to isolate the complexity of various parts of the application server and to optimize startup speed along the way.

There are also countless examples of applications built on top of OSGi. Just like with most other technology, it is hard to find exact usage numbers, but there is a very active user base. The authors of this book use OSGi as the primary technology for most of their projects, including some very large, high-profile applications.

Tooling

In the past few years, a lot of progress has been made on OSGi tooling. When considering a good tool for OSGi development, we have a list of requirements it should take care of:

- Automatically generate bundle JAR files
- Generate package imports using byte code analysis
- Provide an easy way to start an OSGi container to run and test our code
- Hot code updates in a running container for a fast development turnaround
- Run in-container integration tests
- Help with versioning of bundles

Bndtools

Bndtools is by far the tool that fits these requirements best, and we strongly advise using Bndtools for OSGi development. Bndtools is an Eclipse plug-in focused on OSGi development. Under the hood, it's based on BND. BND is a library and set of command-line tools to facilitate OSGi development. Bndtools brings this to the Eclipse IDE. When using Bndtools, you don't have to use Maven for builds, although there is some integration. Bndtools instead generates ANT build files that can be used out of the box for headless/offline builds on a build server, for example. Bndtools also provides wizards for editing manifest files and supports repositories.

Similar to Maven, Bndtools supports the concept of repositories. Repositories are basically a place where bundles are stored and indexed. A Maven repository needs external metadata (the POM file), however; while in OSGi, the metadata is already included in the bundle itself. A repository in Bndtools contains OSGi bundles that you can use within your project. We will delve deeper into using and setting up repositories later.

The most appealing feature of Bndtools is running an OSGi container directly from the IDE enabling hot code updates. This improves development speed enormously and would almost justify the use of OSGi by itself. We will use Bndtools in the remainder of this book, and we strongly recommend you do so as well.

Maven with the BND Maven Plug-in

The BND Maven plug-in can generate bundles and calculate package imports directly from a Maven build. Similar to Bndtools, the plug-in is based on the underlying BND library, and the code analysis used to generate package imports is the same. Other manifest details such as the bundle name and version are extracted from the POM file. This works fine, and many projects use this approach. The major downside is Maven itself. Maven is a decent build tool, but it does a very bad job at facilitating the development process. Fast development requires a fast turnaround of code changes, and this is very difficult to achieve with Maven. Because OSGi bundles already contain all the metadata required to setup dependencies, etc., there is actually no real reason to still use Maven.

Eclipse Tycho

Eclipse Tycho is another Eclipse plug-in that facilitates OSGi development. It is more tied toward Eclipse plug-in development and less fit for general OSGi development. Tycho is also more an addition to Maven than a complete development environment. It helps, for example, to build p2 installation sites, which again is very Eclipse specific.

NetBeans and IntelliJ

NetBeans currently offers only very basic support for OSGi as described on the NetBeans Wiki (*http://bit.ly/18lcK5k*). IntelliJ doesn't offer support for OSGi out-of-the-box. However, both IDEs support Maven, and using the Maven Bundle plug-in, you can develop OSGi projects in a very similar way like any other types of Maven-based projects. Although this works just as well as other types of Java projects, this model misses features such as dynamic bundle reloads and editors for bundle descriptors that Bndtools offers. Without those features, the development experience is simply much less, and you simply don't get all the potential out of OSGi. Even if you are a NetBeans or IntelliJ user, we recommend trying Bndtools with Eclipse. Hopefully, OSGi support in NetBeans and IntelliJ will improve in the near future.

CHAPTER 2

Basic Concepts of OSGi

In this chapter, we will start to go through some basic OSGi concepts. While we want to get you writing useful code as soon as possible, it is helpful to know what is going on behind the scenes.

Hiding Implementations

As discussed in Chapter 1, one of the most important concepts for achieving modularity is to promote cohesion and prevent coupling. For code that you write yourself, this is easy; just don't use implementation classes. For code written by others, this is a lot more difficult. How do you know what code is implementation code in the first place? Java comes up short here. Of course we have access modifiers in Java, but they are defined in a way that makes them hardly usable in a modularity context.

Within parts of an application, there is always some coupling between classes. This is fine, as long as those classes together are usable as a cohesive module. If there would be no coupling at all, it would be impossible to create any useful code. To be able to use other classes, these classes effectively must be *public* in Java. Although there are access modifiers like *private* and *protected*, these access modifiers don't support the concept of isolating modules. They either constrain usage within a module too much or don't constrain external usage sufficiently.

If classes within a module are public, how do we prevent classes that are not part of the module to accidentally use implementation classes? How do we make sure that the cohesion of a module is not broken by not using its public interface? An often-used solution is some kind of package-naming scheme, with package names like "internal" to communicate that certain classes are not meant to be used. There is no way to actually enforce this, and to prevent someone from accidentally using the classes anyway (code completion works against us here). Physically separating APIs from implementations in different JARs (using Maven, for example) does make the situation a lot better but still relies on naming schemes and doesn't solve the runtime modularity question.

Wouldn't it be much more convenient to make classes public within a module but hide them from other modules by default? Classes that should be shared with other modules should be "exported" explicitly. This is exactly what we do in OSGi. In OSGi, a module is packaged in a *bundle*. A bundle is a JAR file with some extra metadata in it, the bundle *manifest*. The manifest contains the name and version of the module and specifies which packages are imported and exported.

Figure 2-1 shows three bundles (modules). Bundle A contains both private and exported packages. This is common for bundles that export their API and contain a default implementation as well. Bundle B only exports a package; it doesn't contain any private packages. This is common for API bundles—bundles that only contain API classes to be implemented by other bundles. Bundle C is the opposite of that: it contains only a private implementation package, maybe implementing the API exported by Bundle B. The bundles can explicitly import packages exported by other bundles.

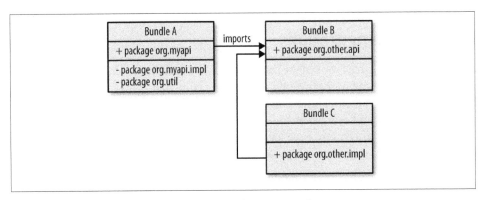

Figure 2-1. Bundles explicitly importing and exporting classes

With a bundle mechanism like this, we can now hide implementations from other bundles. To do this, we need some implementation of an interface to be invoked when one module uses another module. If the implementation is completely hidden, there is no way that another module can instantiate and use that implementation. To solve this problem, we use the well known Inversion of Control pattern. Inversion of control means that some other party is responsible for creating instances and making them available to consumers. Such a party could even be a dependency injection framework such as CDI (Context and Dependency Injection), for example. OSGi itself already has a mechanism for this: OSGi Services, or µservices as they are sometimes called. A service provider registers an implementation for a specific interface as a service to the OSGi Service Registry. A service consumer simply looks up the service in the service registry, using the interface of the required service. The service registry is conceptually the same as the BeanManager in CDI or Spring.

Figure 2-2 shows how a service is registered to the service registry. A service can be looked up by a consumer in the service registry by its service interface. Alternatively, the service registry can notify consumers that certain services are registered or deregistered.

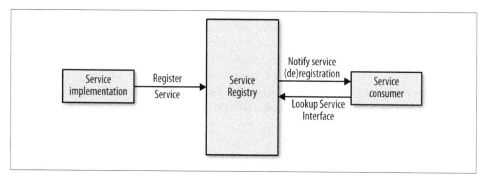

Figure 2-2. Service registration and lookup

The rules of the game are as follows:

1. Service APIs and API classes are exported.
2. Implementation classes are not exported and are therefore not visible to other modules.
3. A service provider registers an implementation in the Service Registry (using a DI framework).
4. A service consumer uses a DI framework to inject service implementations, using only service APIs.

Note that services are available within a single OSGi framework, within a single Java Virtual Machine. There is no remoting or any kind of inter Virtual Machine communication. Service invocations are direct method calls; no proxies or other indirections are used. This makes the runtime overhead of services close to zero. In a real application, you could easily have hundreds of services, and this isn't any kind of performance problem at all. In other words, there is really no reason to avoid the use of services.

These concepts are all we need to achieve basic modularity. Of course there are more advanced patterns and details to discuss, but the basics are as simple as described above.

We will put this to practice soon, but first we need some more basic details about dealing with bundles in OSGi.

About Services

Many people think that services are complex and something you would only need in very advanced situations. Wrong! Services are the basic element of modular applications and are not harder to use than any dependency injection framework. The OSGi specification only provides a low-level API for services. Registering and looking up services is relatively complex using this low-level API, especially concerning service dynamics and thread safety (more about that later). Not to worry, however, unless you are writing low-level libraries, you are not supposed to use these low-level APIs! Instead, you should use one of the available dependency injection frameworks, such as Apache Felix Dependency Manager or Declarative Services, to do the hard work for you.

Import Package Myths

Defining package imports with OSGi is often considered cumbersome. As stated before, each class that should be imported from another module should be explicitly imported in the manifest (the bundle metadata). Doing so by hand would be an extremely tedious task, and for some reason, people are actually trying this. Package imports should be generated from your code. If you start using a new package in code, a new package import header should be generated automatically. Of course, you do have to be careful what packages you use in your code: you don't want your bundle to depend on too many other packages. This isn't any different from controlling your build path as you would do in a normal Java application. Take care when adding new dependencies to your build path.

Depending on Other Modules

We discussed taking care to not depend on too many other packages. However, what is considered "too much"? This is a continuous trade-off. One of the benefits of modularity is potentially better reuse of modules. This is obviously a good thing. Reusing and thereby depending on too many other modules will make the module itself harder to use because you would have to drag in all its dependencies as well. It strongly depends on how the module is intended. Is it a general purpose library that could be used in any kind of application, or is it a module very specific for a certain application? General purpose modules are easier to use when there are fewer dependencies. As with many things in software, there is no strict right or wrong.

Service Dynamics

Having a modular runtime, it is possible to activate and deactive modules (bundles) at runtime. One example where this could happen is when a bundle is being updated; it must be restarted to activate changes. This doesn't matter for the classloading and re-solving process in OSGi. Once a class is loaded by a bundle, it will stay that way until that bundle is reinstalled itself. Services are an entirely different story, however; services are dynamic. Dynamic means that a service can be registered or deregistered at any moment during runtime, and we have to deal with the possibility that a service dissappears during invocation. A service invocation can throw an exception during invocation if the underlying service has become deregistered, and our code has to handle this correctly. This is very similar to invoking code that uses external components such as a database.

To complicate things further, we have to deal with thread safety. You can start your own threads in an OSGi container, and the OSGi container might use different threads to register and deregister services. This means there could be multiple threads that use a service when it is being deregistered. Dealing with this by hand is complicated because it requires nontrivial locking code, but once again, the dependency injection frameworks solve this entirely for us.

Service dynamics also give us a lot of flexibility. We have different options to choose from when dealing with service dependencies that are not available. If one service requires another service to do its work (e.g., a business logic service that requires a Data Access Object), it might define a dependency as *required*. When the other service is unregistered, and therefore becomes unavailable, the service with the now unavailable dependency can automatically be deregistered as well. Of course this degrades the application's functionality, but this might be perfectly fine during maintenance windows. Other parts of the application can continue to work as normal. In other cases, a service might continue to be available even when its dependencies are not available. A trivial example is a dependency on a log service. Even without logging, you can execute most code. Another solution might be to inform a user that specific functionality is currently unavailable. The last option is to dynamically switch to another implementation (or version) of the same service interface. This way we have a mechanism of "graceful degradation" in place that enables hot system updates. We are going to see examples of all approaches in the remainder of this book.

Developers coming from Java EE often wonder why you would want dynamic services in the first place. Service dynamics add some complexity because you always have to be aware of the fact that services can become unavailable. The reason dynamic services are worth the extra complexity is that they give very powerful deployment and update possibilities. Because Java EE is static by nature, you always have to completely undeploy an entire application before you can install updates. With a dynamic services framework, such as OSGi, we can install updates of single modules without taking the system down.

This is a very powerful deployment mechanism that changes the way to deal with software updates completely. Besides updates, dynamic services also come in to play when configuration of a system is changed, for example; the system can dynamically reconfigure itself without taking it down.

The Bundle Format

A *bundle* is the deployment unit in OSGi. Basically, a bundle is just a JAR file with a bundle *manifest*. The manifest itself is a file named *META-INF/MANIFEST.MF*. We will describe the most important headers in the manifest here, but remember that you will normally not write this by hand.

Bundle-SymbolicName

This is the formal name of the bundle. It may not contain spaces. Although not technically required, it is common to use the following format:

```
com.mycompany.project.somebundle.api
```

A real-word example would be the Apache Felix HTTP Service implementation:

```
org.apache.felix.http.jetty
```

Bundle-Name

The *Bundle-Name* is a user friendly name. You will see this name, for example, when you list bundles in an OSGi console (depending on what console you use). This name may contain spaces. The *Bundle-SymbolicName* and *Bundle-Name* are technically unrelated. When no *Bundle-Name* is specified, most consoles and other tools will fall back to the *Bundle-SymbolicName*.

Bundle-Version

The *Bundle-Version* is the version of the bundle itself. The first thing to remember is that this version is not used for importing/exporting classes and interfaces. Importing and exporting is done using the *Import-Package* and *Export-Package* headers instead.

This makes the *Bundle-Version* technically not that interesting, but it is still important while releasing bundles and communicating version numbers to users.

In OSGi, the following versioning scheme is used:

```
major.minor.micro
```

Major, minor, and *micro* are numeric values. In some cases, a fourth part is used, the *qualifier.* This is often a build number or a date. A qualifier can be alphanumeric. For example:

```
1.1.2.4121232
```

Import-Package

Import-Package (together with *Export-Package*) is one of the most important manifest headers in OSGi. With an import, you define a dependency on a specific package and make the classes and interfaces in that package available to your bundle. Only explicitly exported packages (see *Export-Package*) are available for import.

It's only possible to load classes in a bundle when they are explicitly imported. If classes that are not imported are used, a *ClassNotFoundException* will occur. This may sound very fragile, and it's even one of the often-heard arguments about why OSGi would be too difficult to use. You should never write package imports by hand, however, but leave this to build tooling. BND is the most commonly used tool for this. BND generates package imports by performing byte code analysis. If BND is used to build bundles, the bundle will always have the correct import manifest headers. When using Bndtools, which we strongly advise in this book, this will all happen completely automatic. Alternatively, BND can also be integrated in Maven or ANT, if Bndtools is not used.

When a bundle is installed in an OSGi framework, the framework will try to resolve the imported packages defined by the bundle. If there are import package statements defined that are not exported by any of the other installed bundles, the bundle will not be started, and the framework will warn about the unresolved package. As soon as another bundle is installed that does export the package, the framework resolves the bundle that could not be started earlier. When resolving is successful, the bundle can be started; the framework will not automatically do this, however.

The resolver is a very important mechanism when using OSGi. Instead of running into classloading exceptions during runtime because of a missing dependency, we will learn about missing dependencies as soon as we install our bundles. This is a great benefit compared to non-OSGi Java applications.

Assuming that we import all packages that we use in our code, by using BND, the resolver will protect us from most cases of class loading exceptions. There is one case where BND will actually not generate the correct imports, which will lead to runtime *Class NotFoundExceptions.* BND will not generate import headers for classes loaded using *Class.forName().* Because classes loaded this way are not part of the byte code, BND won't see them. The easiest workaround is to manually add the import header, but for more dynamic scenarios, there are other solutions that will be discussed in "Dynamic Classloading" on page 86.

When importing a package, we can specify a version range. Only exported packages that are within the version range will be used by the resolver. Package versions use the same versioning scheme as bundles: *major.minor.micro*. A version can be explicit, such as 1.1.2, but more often, a range of versions is specified. A version range can be used to be compatible with any version in the same major range, for example. Table 2-1 contains some examples of version ranges.

Table 2-1. Examples of version ranges

Version range	Description
version="1.1.2"	This version and up to infinity
version="[1,2)"	Equal or higher than 1.0.0, lower than 2.0.0
version="[1.1,1.9]"	Equal or higher than 1.1.0, equal or lower than 1.9.x
version="[1.1,1.9.3]"	Equal or higher than 1.1.0, equal or lower than 1.9.3
version="(1.1.1,1.9.3)"	Higher than 1.1.1, lower than 1.9.3
version="(1.1.1,1.9.3]"	Higher than 1.1.1, equal or lower than 1.9.3

Version ranges work very well if the exported package uses "semantic versioning." This is a set of rules that define what kinds of code changes should result in a major, minor, or micro version update. We will see a lot more about semantic versioning in "Semantic Versioning" on page 45.

At first it might seem too fine-grained to import every package that you depend upon. As an alternative, developers often look at the Require-Bundle header, which allows you to depend on a specific bundle as a whole. This is considered to be a bad practice, and you should not use it. Depending on individual packages makes it possible to resolve against different sources of an exported package, which removes coupling between specific bundles; the package can be imported from any bundle that exports the package.

Export-Package

Export-Package is the opposite of Import-Package. It is used to make a package available to be imported by other bundles. Only explicitly exported packages are available for import, so it is required to export packages that should be available to others. Only classes and interfaces that are part of an API should be exported. Implementation classes (including default implementations) should always be hidden.

A package export is always versioned (0.0.0 by default). As discussed in the section about Import-Package, a package import should be versioned to specify compatibility with different versions of an API. This is obviously only possible when the exporting package specifies a version. The syntax of an Export-Package is as follows:

```
Export-Package: com.example.api;version="1.0"
```

An Export-Package header can specify a uses constraint. This can be used to define transitive dependencies on other packages so that an importing bundle knows about the extra package requirements imposed by importing a specific package. An example is our *com.example.api* package, which depends on another package, *com.some-other.api*.

```
Export-Package: com.example.api;version="1.0";uses:="com.someother.api"
```

Note that BND will automatically generate uses constraints. It will analyze all the code within the exported package, and generate uses constraints for all required import packages for that code.

Bundle-Activator

A Bundle-Activator is a class that implements the BundleActivator interface and will be instantiated and invoked by the OSGi framework when the bundle is started or stopped. An activator must have a no-arg constructor so that the framework can instantiate it. In most common cases, an activator is used to register services and define dependencies on other services. The Activator class doesn't have to (and should not) be exported. We do need to reference it in the manifest headers, however:

```
Bundle-Activator: com.example.osgi.ExampleActivator
```

The activator itself could be implemented as follows:

```java
import org.osgi.framework.BundleActivator;
import org.osgi.framework.BundleContext;

public class Activator implements BundleActivator {

    @Override
    public void start(BundleContext context) throws Exception {
        System.out.println("Bundle starting");
    }

    @Override
    public void stop(BundleContext context) throws Exception {
        System.out.println("Bundle stopping");
    }
}
```

We will start using activators as soon a we start building our first bundles in the next chapter.

Running an OSGi Application

In this book, we will see several ways to run or deploy OSGi applications. Using tooling, this can be as simple as clicking a button. To understand what happens, it is good to have some insights in what an OSGi container is exactly, and how you start one.

When starting an OSGi application, the following happens:

- The OSGi container is started.
- Bundles are installed into the container.
- Bundles are resolved by the container.
- Bundle activators are invoked. This is where your code "starts."

We can easily start an OSGi container from Java code. In the following example, an OSGi framework is started, and three bundles are installed into it. When executing this code, you would have a running OSGi application that shows an OSGi shell (provided by the Apache Felix Gogo bundles). On the classpath, you would need an OSGi framework implementation such as Apache Felix. The three bundles in the example are loaded from the filesystem:

```java
import java.util.ArrayList;
import java.util.HashMap;
import java.util.List;
import java.util.Map;
import java.util.ServiceLoader;

import org.osgi.framework.Bundle;
import org.osgi.framework.BundleContext;
import org.osgi.framework.BundleException;
import org.osgi.framework.launch.Framework;
import org.osgi.framework.launch.FrameworkFactory;

public class LauncherExample {
    public static void main(String args[]) throws BundleException {
        FrameworkFactory frameworkFactory = ServiceLoader
            .load(FrameworkFactory.class).iterator().next();
        Map<String, String> config = new HashMap<>();
        Framework framework = frameworkFactory.newFramework(config);
        framework.start();

        BundleContext context = framework.getBundleContext();
        List<Bundle> bundles = new ArrayList<>();
        bundles.add(

context.installBundle("file:org.apache.felix.gogo.command-0.10.0.jar"));
        bundles.add(
```

```
context.installBundle("file:org.apache.felix.gogo.runtime-0.10.0.jar"));
        bundles.add(

context.installBundle("file:org.apache.felix.gogo.shell-0.10.0.jar"));

        for (Bundle bundle : bundles) {
            bundle.start();
        }
    }
}
```

The launcher API is part of the OSGi specification and works across implementations. Because an OSGi framework can be started from code, it is easy to imagine different ways an OSGi framework could be used or embedded. For most situations, you won't need to create a launcher yourself. In the remainder of the book, we will look at several ways to run OSGi code using existing launchers and containers.

The Framework Lifecycle

The framework and bundles have their own individual lifecycle. Figure 2-3 shows the framework lifecycle with the different states a bundle goes through.

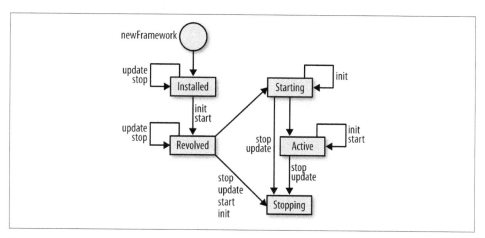

Figure 2-3. Framework lifecycle

The following list describes the different bundle states. It's important to understand these states. Every time a bundle is updated, it goes through the different states. While working in Bndtools with a running framework, this even happens at every code change. In production systems, it is also common to update single bundles in a running framework:

Installed
> The bundle is installed into the framework but cannot be started because it can't be resolved (e.g., missing import packages).

Resolved
> The bundle is successfully resolved, but is not started. This is also the state when the bundle is manually stopped.

Starting
> The bundle is currently starting; the activator init method is invoked.

Active
> The bundle is functioning; its services can be used by other bundles.

Stopping
> The bundle is currently stopping; the activator destroy method is invoked.

The *installed* state is an interesting one. When a bundle stays in the installed state, it almost always means something is wrong with the deployment; the bundle can't be started because it is missing dependencies. This should be the first thing to check after starting or updating a framework when the application doesn't start correctly.

When a bundle is installed or updated, it is automatically started if it resolved correctly. When a bundle does not resolve, it stays in the installed state. It will never be started automatically, not even when the missing constraints are fixed. Instead it will remain in the resolved state until it is explicitly started. This behavior is according to specification but unexpected for some users.

CHAPTER 3

Creating the First OSGi Application

Throughout the rest of this book, we will build a simple, conference-scheduling application as an example. Along the way, we will add a NoSQL datastore, create RESTful web services, and deploy it to the cloud. Because long code listings in a book don't read very well, we keep all code examples short. You can download the full source code from GitHub (*http://bit.ly/14DTna9*).

In this chapter, we will create the following parts of the application:

- An API bundle containing our domain classes and service API
- An OSGi service
- A Gogo shell command that uses our service

Figure 3-1 depicts the application as a set of bundles. By developing it this way, you will get some hands-on experience with creating bundles, package imports, and exports; creating services; and running applications from Bndtools.

Prerequisites

Before you get started, make sure you have all prerequisites installed:

- A Java Development Kit (JDK 7 or higher).
- Eclipse, with the Bndtools plug-in installed. The book examples are written using Bndtools 2.x. Bndtools can be installed from the Eclipse Marketplace.

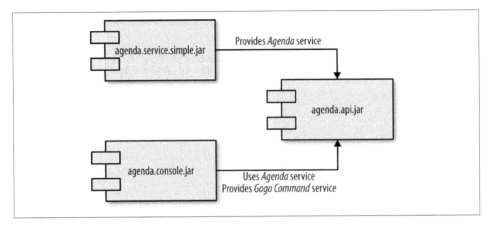

Figure 3-1. Overview of the agenda application

Getting Started

After installing and starting Eclipse, let's start working on the example application by creating a new project using the Eclipse Bndtools plug-in. Start with an empty workspace, and create a new Bndtools OSGi project. The project name should be agenda. Click Next and choose Empty Project on the next screen and click Finish. Bndtools will now ask if you want to create a cnf project. The cnf project contains configuration for repositories and all your other projects in the workspace. A repository contains the bundles that you depend on, such as frameworks and libraries. You can compare a bundle repository to a Maven repository; it contains JAR files with metadata. The metadata for a Maven JAR file is in the *pom.xml*, and the metadata for an OSGi bundle is in the bundle's manifest file. Accept the default to create the cnf project.

 Bndtools assumes a workspace is created for a set of related bundles. If you are building an application, it should have it's own workspace. You shouldn't put projects from different applications in the same workspace.

The agenda project is almost a plain Java project. There is a *bnd.bnd* file (which in fact is a plain text file containing BND configuration) and an Ant *build.xml* file. The *bnd.bnd* file contains all the bundle configuration, the Ant file is for building the project on a build server. Bndtools uses bnd files to specify manifest information. While Bndtools generates most of the information or provides wizards to edit the values, you can always edit the bnd files yourself.

The cnf project in the workspace, created by Bndtools, should be checked in into version control as well. The same goes for Eclipse *.project* files. This is the only way to get a seamless check-out experience when starting with a new workspace.

Creating an API Bundle

In Bndtools, you can choose to create an Eclipse project per bundle, or create several bundles in a single Eclipse project. Multiple bundles in a single Eclipse project share the same build path (your compile path), which has no effect on the bundle output but is easy to work with in Eclipse. The guideline is to put bundles that are functionally related in the same Eclipse project. We are going to start by creating an API bundle. An API bundle contains exported/public classes and interfaces but should not contain implementations. Start by creating a new bundle descriptor in the agenda project, and name it api. If Bndtools asks to enable sub-bundles, accept the default (yes) and click Finish. If you take a look in the generated folder, there should now be an empty JAR file *agenda.api.jar*. Double-click to open the JAR File Viewer and inspect to see if it is really empty. The JAR File Viewer is a handy tool that might come of use later on. Next, add a new class agenda.api.Conference and a new interface agenda.api.Agenda. The Conference class should have the following properties and getters/setters:

```
String name;
String location;
```

Also, implement a no-argument constructor and a convenience constructor that accepts name and location as parameters. The Agenda interface should have two methods:

```
List<Conference> listConferences();
void addConference(Conference conference);
```

We should now add these API classes to the bundle. Open the *api.bnd* file and drag the *agenda.api* package to the Exported Packages area. Bndtools will prompt for a version for the export package; select the default 1.0.0. This version will be part of the Export-Package definition. Save the *api.bnd* file and take another look at the generated JAR file using the JAR File Viewer. It should now contain the Conference class and the Agenda interface. The *META-INF/MANIFEST.MF* file should now contain an export header:

```
Export-Package: agenda.api;version="1.0"
```

You are now done creating your first bundle. The agenda.api can now be used by other bundles. As you can see, Bndtools took care of generating the JAR file and generating the manifest, based on information provided in the *bnd.bnd* file.

You will notice that the *Bundle-SymbolicName* of a Bndtools bundle is derived from the project name plus (optionally) the bundle descriptor name. In most cases, the familiar reverse domain name naming convention is used; e.g., `org.apache.felix.dm`. For brevity, the examples in this book do not use that convention.

Creating an OSGi Service

Now that there is a simple interface, we can create the first OSGi service that implements the `Agenda` interface. It should be packaged in a separate bundle so that we can easily switch implementations. Create another bundle by creating a new bundle descriptor named `service.simple`. Now add a new class, `agenda.service.simple.Simple AgendaService`, which implements the `Agenda` interface. This implementation of the agenda should store conferences in-memory, so you can simply use a thread-safe list to store the conferences. For example:

```
private List<Conference> conferences = new CopyOnWriteArrayList<>();
```

Implement both interface methods by simply returning the conferences list and adding a new conference to the list.

The first `Agenda` service implementation is now completed. As you can see, the service implementation is just plain Java, nothing fancy or OSGi related required. We do have to register the service into the OSGi Service Registry, however. OSGi has a low-level API for this, but you shouldn't use this when doing application development. Instead, you should use a dependency injection framework to do so. There are several choices, such as *Apache Felix Dependency Manager*, *Declarative Services*, and *BluePrint*. These frameworks offer different ways to do roughly the same thing: publish services in the service registry and use services from the service registry. There are some differences, however, and choosing a framework is mostly dependent on preference for writing Java code, annotations, or XML. In the remainder of this book, we will use Apache Felix Dependency Manager. This is one of the oldest dependency injection frameworks for OSGi and is still the most powerful, with some features not present in alternatives. Some of the advanced features, such as *Aspect Services*, will be used in Chapter 4. Apache Felix Dependency Manager has support for a Java API and annotations. Throughout the book, we will mostly use the Java API.

When to Use the Low-Level API

In most cases, you should use a dependency injection framework to publish and consume OSGi services. Even when, depending on the framework, there are no compile time dependencies on the framework, there will always be a runtime dependency. This means that a user of your bundle must include the dependency injection runtime bundle(s) in his runtime as well. When doing application development, this is a very small cost. When creating general purpose libraries or frameworks aimed to be used in any kind of application, this might be a problem. A user of your library or framework will not be happy to pull in several other dependencies together with the library you created.

In these cases, it's a more difficult trade-off, which should be carefully considered. More information about using the low-level API to produce and consume services can be found in "The Low-Level Service API" on page 82.

To start using Apache Felix Dependency Manager, we first have to add it to the build path of the project. Because Apache Felix Dependency Manager is not in our bundle repository yet, we will first have to add it there. You can download dependencies from the various projects manually and drag them into your *local* repository.

Download the following bundles from *http://felix.apache.org/site/downloads.cgi*:

- Dependency Manager
- Dependency Manager Shell

Drag both JAR files from your download folder to the Local repository in the Repositories view in the lower left corner of your screen (make sure the Bndtools Perspective is open). In case you don't see the Local Repository in the Repositories viewer, press the green refresh icon and try again. Now open the *bnd.bnd* file of the agenda project and go to the Build tab. Click the green "plus" button and select the following bundles:

- `org.apache.felix.dependencymanager`
- `osgi.core`

Using Repositories to Find Bundles

When creating real applications, you will generally use several existing components. You can find and download or build the binaries for these components yourself on the various project websites. However, this can be a tedious job if you require several of them.

To make this easier, Bndtools supports the concept of repositories. A repository is conceptually any place where bundles can be stored, and there are several repository implementations available. Several parties host online repositories that you can use to easily find bundles. One of these parties is the Amdatu project. Amdatu is an open source project that contains components focused at build modular *cloud* applications. We will discuss Amdatu in much more detail later in this book, but the repositories are useful right now. All libraries used in this book can be found in the Amdatu repositories.

A repository can be configured in Bndtools using the Bndtools → Open ext/ repositories.bnd.

Copy the repositories described at the Amdatu website to the *-plugin* section (*http://bit.ly/15kjs9Q*). Make sure there are no dangling spaces.

If you now refresh the repositories view in Bndtools, you should see two new repositories containing many different bundles. These are not only Amdatu bundles, but also bundles from Apache Felix and other often-used bundles.

Don't forget to save afterward. Registering a service is done in a bundle `Activator`. This is a class that will be invoked by the OSGi container when the bundle is started and stopped. Create a new class `agenda.service.simple.Activator` that extends `Depend encyActivatorBase`, which is a base class from Apache Felix Dependency Manager. Implement the `init` method as follows:

```
manager.add(createComponent()
    .setInterface(Agenda.class.getName(), null)
    .setImplementation(SimpleAgendaService.class));
```

Apache Felix Dependency Manager will register the `SimpleAgendaService` as an `Agenda` OSGi service. From now on, the service can be injected into other components. Apache Felix Dependency Manager will take care of all the hairy details with thread safeness. It will also automatically cleanly deregister the service when the bundle is stopped; we don't have to write any code for this.

We still have to add the newly created classes to the `service.simple` bundle. Open the *service.simple.bnd* file and drag the `agenda.service.simple` package to the Private Packages area. The classes are now added to the bundle JAR file but will not be exported. Other bundles will not be able to see or use the classes, and that's exactly what we want. Implementation classes should be hidden from other bundles; only APIs should be shared. We also have to configure the `Activator` in the manifest. You can do this on the Contents tab of the *services.simple.bnd* file. In the top left corner, select your newly created `Activator` class from the drop-down list. Save and you are all set with your first OSGi service.

Running the Code

Now that we have a service, it would be interesting to actually run the code. Running an OSGi application is done by starting an OSGi framework with our application bundles and all dependent bundles installed. Bndtools makes this very easy. Open the *bnd.bnd* file and go to the Run tab. First we need to specify the OSGi Framework that we will be using. Choose Apache Felix from the drop-down list, and set the Java execution environment to the Java version you are using. On the righthand side, you will see Run Requirements and Run Bundles. The Run Bundles is a list of bundles that will be installed when you run the application. You shouldn't edit this list by hand in most cases, but use the Run Requirements instead. In the Run Requirements, you specify a list of bundles that you need to run the application. A resolver will then be used to calculate which other bundles you depend on. This is calculated using the imports of the bundles. The disadvantage of this is that only dependencies that you compile against (APIs, for example) will be resolved. Bundles that only provide services, such as the `agenda.services.simple` bundle, cannot be resolved, and you will have to add them yourself to the Run Requirements. Bundles in the current project will be added automatically.

Use the small brick with green plus icon to add the following list of bundles to the Run Requirements:

- `org.apache.felix.gogo.command`
- `org.apache.felix.gogo.runtime`
- `org.apache.felix.gogo.shell`
- `org.apache.felix.dependencymanager`
- `org.apache.felix.dependencymanager.shell`
- `osgi.cmpn`

Gogo is an OSGi console that you can use to see the list of installed bundles, stop and start bundles, view the log, etc. The Dependency Manager Shell is a shell command that gives you an overview of services and service dependencies. This is a great debugging tool when a service doesn't start.

After adding the bundles to the Required Bundles list, you can click the Resolve button and save the bnd file. Make sure you explicitly save every time you make a change to the bnd configuration. Changes will only be picked up after you save the configuration. Now start the framework by clicking the green Run OSGi button. In the Eclipse console, you will now see the OSGi shell. You can view the list of installed bundles by typing **lb** in the console window. The bundle state should be `ACTIVE` for all bundles. This means the bundles are started and all required imports are resolved. If, for example, you would remove the dependency manager bundle, the `agenda.simple.service` bundle would remain in `INSTALLED` state (you can try this without even restarting the framework). `INSTALLED` means that the bundle has not or could not be started because some imported packages could not be resolved. You can explicitly stop and start bundles with the **stop** and **start** commands.

When a bundle is `ACTIVE`, it only says that all imports have been resolved and the `BundleActivator`'s start method has been invoked. It doesn't say anything about the availability of services it might register. Services are dynamic and can be registered and unregistered while the bundle is `ACTIVE`, even without restarting the bundle. You can get more information about registered services and dependencies between services by using the `dm` command. For example, you could look up the id of the `agenda.service.simple` service using the `lb` command and then type `dm [id]`. It should show something similar to this:

```
[9] agenda.service.simple
    agenda.api.Agenda() registered
```

Our Agenda service implementation is not doing much yet; it's registered, but nobody is using it. Let's start by adding some test data to the list of conferences when the service starts. For this, you can add a start method to the service implementation class. This is an Apache Felix Dependency Manager specific lifecycle method, but most alternative frameworks support something similar. Here is what an example start method might look like:

```
public void start() {
    conferences.add(new Conference("Devoxx", "Antwerp"));
    conferences.add(new Conference("Jfokus", "Stockholm"));

    System.out.println("Added " + conferences.size() + " conferences");
}
```

After saving your code changes, take a look at the console. What does it say?

Using the Agenda Service

Let's create a consumer for the Agenda service. We will create a RESTful web service on top of the Agenda service later on in the lab, but for now, we will keep things within the OSGi shell. We will create a shell command that we can use from the OSGi shell to add and list conferences. Note that the OSGi shell is not meant to be used as an end-user shell. It's just useful for debugging purposes, but we can now use it to test interaction with our Agenda service.

Create a new bundle descriptor named console. Add a new class agenda.console. AgendaConsole. This class doesn't implement or extend any interfaces or base classes, it's just a POJO. First we will add an instance field for the Agenda service dependency:

```
private volatile Agenda agenda;
```

Please note the usage of the Java volatile keyword. This is a recommended practice, as the reference will be injected by the Apache Felix Dependency Manager and because of service dynamics, it might or might not be there at a given point in time. By making it *volatile*, we ensure that changes are immediately visible in all threads that might be using it. We will further explore service dynamics later on. Next, add two methods that will be invoked by the shell:

```
public void listConferences() {
    List<Conference> conferences = agenda.listConferences();

    for (Conference conference : conferences) {
        System.out.println(conference.getName());
    }
}
```

```
public void addConference(String name, String location) {
    agenda.addConference(new Conference(name, location));
}
```

The reference to the Agenda service should be looked up from the service registry. Just as with service registration, you should use a dependency injection framework for this instead of using the low-level APIs. The low-level APIs require you to deal with the hairy details of figuring out when all dependencies become available. Remember that services can come and go at any time. This is nontrivial and a lot of work. With a dependency injection framework, it's very easy, however, as the framework will take care of the dynamics. To do so, we have to register the component and declare a dependency on the Agenda service. We will do so in a new Activator class. However, our shell command doesn't have a Java interface. It's just a POJO, so the *interface* of our service will be Object.class. This is to say that our component has the lifecycle of a service, but is not meant to be used from other Java classes. How does our command get registered in the shell then? For that, we use so-called *service properties* to flag the service as a command:

```
@Override
public void init(BundleContext context, DependencyManager manager)
        throws Exception {
    Properties props = new Properties();
    props.put(CommandProcessor.COMMAND_SCOPE, "agenda");
    props.put(CommandProcessor.COMMAND_FUNCTION, new String[] {
            "listConferences", "addConference" });

    manager.add(createComponent()
        .setInterface(Object.class.getName(), props)
        .setImplementation(AgendaConsole.class)
        .add(createServiceDependency()
            .setService(Agenda.class)));
}
```

To be able to use the Gogo CommandProcessor, we need to add org.apache.felix.go go.runtime to our build path. Gogo will pick up any service that has the CommandPro cessor service properties and register the service as a shell command. This is "whiteboard style" registration, and you will see several implementations of this pattern throughout the book. Finally, add the agenda.console package to the *console.bnd* Private Packages, and don't forget to configure the Activator.

As soon as you save the *console.bnd* file, you should be able to see the new bundle with lb if the framework is still running. This is one of the great things of working with OSGi and Bndtools: hot code deployments and (almost) never restarting a server.

Type **help** in the console. You should see the two new commands in the list of commands. Try adding a conference by typing the following command:

```
addConference JavaOne SanFrancisco
```

And try listing conferences to see if it worked:

```
listConferences
```

With the three bundles completed, we now have the structure depicted in Figure 3-2.

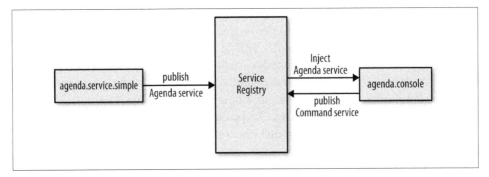

Figure 3-2. Service interaction via the service registry

Service Instances

OSGi services are effectively singletons. A registered service represents a single service instance, and this instance is shared by all consumers of the service. This has several implications:

- Services must be thread safe.
- Services can be used to share state.
- It's impossible to create service instances for specific clients.

This model is similar to a lot of other frameworks, including servlets, EJB Singleton Beans, and Spring beans (by default). Most important, you should always make sure service code is thread safe.

A new OSGi enterprise specification, RFC-195 Service Scopes, is in development and adds a "prototype" scope to services. With prototype services, a new service instance can be created for each client of the service. This would open the doors for more advanced scoping mechanisms as well. It's too early to dive into Service Scopes now, but it could be an interesting addition.

Understanding Service Dynamics

OSGi services are dynamic; they can be registered and deregistered at runtime. What does that mean exactly, and when would that happen? In an OSGi environment, it is perfectly possible to update components or change configuration of a running

---

application. We don't have to take the application down to do the update; this can all be done without ever restarting. We could also start new services when new configuration is added (at runtime), for example. This gives a lot of flexibility when deploying an application, but your code needs to be able to handle this situation.

Let's say that the SimpleAgenda service is being updated. To update the bundle, the bundle has to be stopped, updated, and started again. What happens if some other service (like our command) tries to invoke the Agenda service while the bundle is stopped? We can try this by stopping the agenda.service.simple bundle and then issuing the **listConferences** command.

That will result in a NullPointerException. The reason for that is that by default, Apache Felix Dependency Manager will inject an object that returns null for every method invocation when the service is unavailable. That means that the conferences variable in the following example will be null:

```
List<Conference> conferences = agenda.listConferences();
```

The iteration over this variable will throw the NullPointerException. By default, we will have to handle NullPointerException situations ourselves in case our service dependencies are not available. This is very useful in some cases. In our command, for example, we could return a user-friendly message when the Agenda is not available:

```
public void listConferences() {
    List<Conference> conferences = agenda.listConferences();
    if(conferences != null) {
        for (Conference conference : conferences) {
            System.out.println(conference.getName());
        }
    } else {
        System.out.println("Agenda not available");
    }
}
```

Save your code change and run **listConferences** again in the console. It should now display Agenda not available. Our simple program now gracefully degrades when the agenda service is not available. In many other cases, there is nothing useful you can do when a service you depend on is unavailable, and it would be a lot of work to add extra null checks everywhere in the code. In such cases, it would be much more convenient if the service that requires the unavailable service would also be deregistered. Apache Felix Dependency Manager can do this automatically. All you have to do is to set the service dependency as required in the activator:

```
manager.add(createComponent()
    .setInterface(Object.class.getName(), props)
    .setImplementation(AgendaConsole.class)
    .add(createServiceDependency()
```

```
        .setService(Agenda.class)
        .setRequired(true)));
```

If we stop the `agenda.service.simple` bundle again and use the `listConferences` command, the shell will now show an error that the command doesn't exist. Because the command service has a required dependency on the `Agenda` service, the whole command service itself will be deregistered when the `Agenda` is unavailable. When the `Agenda` service is available again (start the `agenda.service.simple bundle` in the console), the command will automatically register again as well.

Note that the deregistration of the `Agenda` service could potentially happen during the invocation of the `listConferences` method. The service would throw an exception, and our code has to either expect exceptions and deal with them, or accept the fact that invocation might fail. This is the similar to using an external component such as a database.

Services and Bundle States

When a bundle becomes active, it means that all imported packages were resolved and the activator (if there is one) was executed without exceptions. This does not say anything about services. When a bundle is active, it doesn't necessarily mean that the bundle already registered services, and if it did, that the services are registered successfully. This might seem strange at first, but remember that a bundle might register a service at any time during runtime. Services don't have to be registered necessarily during bundle activation, although this is of course a common case. Because the bundle state doesn't give us any information about the state of services, we need some additional tools to debug services.

Debugging Services

We have seen that services can depend on services. Services can also depend on configuration; this will be discussed in "Managed Services" on page 53. Because these dependencies and the dynamic nature of services, it may happen that a service doesn't become available because of a configuration issue, for example. Apache Felix Dependency Manager has some really useful shell commands to debug services. To use these, you obviously need a shell (such as the Apache Felix Gogo shell like we used earlier) and the Apache Felix Dependency Manager shell commands. The latter can be found in the `org.apache.felix.dependencymanager.shell` bundle. After adding this bundle to your runtime, you will have the following commands available:

dm
    Lists all services

dm [bundleId]
    Lists services of a specific bundle

```
dm notavail
```
Lists services that are currently unavailable

The output of these commands includes a dependency graph of the service. This way it is easy to spot problems. The following is an example of a healthy service:

```
[9] agenda.console
    java.lang.Object(osgi.command.function=
        {listConferences,addConference},osgi.command.scope=agenda) registered
    agenda.api.Agenda service required available
[10] agenda.service.simple
    agenda.api.Agenda() registered
```

This example lists services for two bundles: bundle 9 and bundle 10. It shows that bundle 9 published a service with interface `java.lang.Object` (basically no interface) and service properties `osgi.command.function` and `osgi.command.scope`. It also shows that the service has a dependency on `agenda.api.Agenda`, which is currently available. Bundle 10 publishes a service with interface `agenda.api.Agenda`.

If we stop bundle 10, it will deregister the Agenda service. The output for **dm 9** will then be:

```
[9] agenda.console
    java.lang.Object(osgi.command.function=
        {listConferences,addConference},osgi.command.scope=agenda) unregistered
    agenda.api.Agenda service required unavailable
```

It now clearly states that bundle 9 tried to publish a service, but the service did not become available because its required dependency on `agenda.api.Agenda` is not available. When the dependency on `agenda.api.Agenda` were optional, the output would be:

```
[9] agenda.console
    java.lang.Object(osgi.command.function=
        {listConferences,addConference},osgi.command.scope=agenda) registered
    agenda.api.Agenda service optional unavailable
```

It still recognizes that the `agenda.api.Agenda` dependency is not available. Because the dependency is not required, the command is still registered.

The Apache Felix Dependency Manager Shell is a very valuable tool. In a real system, there may be hundreds of services depending on one another and depending on configuration, and Apache Felix Dependency Manager Shell enables us to debug when things don't go as expected.

Having Multiple Service Implementations

It is possible to have multiple implementations of a service in a runtime. Let's take the following interface and implementations as an example:

```
public interface Greeter {
    void sayHello();
}

public class FriendlyGreeter implements Greeter {
    @Override
    public void sayHello() {
        System.out.println("Good morning!")
    }
}

public class GrumpyGreeter implements Greeter {
    @Override
    public void sayHello() {
        System.out.println("Leave me alone!")
    }
}
```

Then we could have another bundle that creates a component that depends on the Greeter service:

```
manager.add(createComponent()
    .setInterface(Object.class.getName(), null)
    .setImplementation(OtherComponent.class)
    .add(createServiceDependency()
        .setService(Greeter.class)));

public class OtherComponent {
    private volatile Greeter greeter;
}
```

When we install all three bundles, it will seem as if the framework will arbitrarily choose one of the implementations of Greeter to inject into OtherComponent. This is not very useful in most cases, but it is interesting what happens when the injected service becomes unavailable: the other service implementation will automatically be injected as a replacement. This way we can deregister a service (e.g., stop the providing bundle) and automatically fall back to another service. This way you can hot-switch between implementations.

This mechanism becomes even more powerful when we can have some more control over it using service properties and service rankings.

Service Properties

When we implemented the Gogo command, we already saw service properties. Service properties are properties added to the service definition, and they can be used to filter services. Let's first add some properties to both of the `Greeter` implementations as an example. This is done when registering the service:

`FriendlyGreeter`:

```
Properties properties = new Properties();
properties.put("greetingType", "friendly");

manager.add(createComponent()
    .setInterface(Greeter.class.getName(), properties)
    .setImplementation(FriendlyGreeter.class);
```

`GrumpyGreeter`:

```
Properties properties = new Properties();
properties.put("greetingType", "grumpy");

manager.add(createComponent()
    .setInterface(Greeter.class.getName(), properties)
    .setImplementation(GrumpyGreeter.class);
```

When injecting the `Greeter` into `OtherComponent`, we can use a service filter to choose an implementation with specific service properties.

`OtherComponent`:

```
manager.add(createComponent()
    .setInterface(Object.class.getName(), null)
    .setImplementation(OtherComponent.class)
    .add(createServiceDependency()
        .setService(Greeter.class, "(greetingType=friendly)")));
```

The magic is in the second parameter of the `setService` method from the Apache Felix Dependency Manager API. We pass the service filter (`greetingType=friendly`), which will make sure we will only inject services matching this filter. The filter syntax is LDAP style. Table 3-1 lists some examples of filters. Note that filter keys are case insensitive.

Table 3-1. Filter examples

Filter	Description
(someproperty=somevalue)	"Equal" value filter
(!(someproperty=somevalue))	"Not" filter
(&((someproperty=somevalue)(someotherproperty=othervalue)))	"And" filter
(|((someproperty=somevalue)(someotherproperty=othervalue)))	"Or" filter
((someproperty=*))	"Any" filter

Service Ranking

A special kind of property is the `service.ranking` property. The higher the ranking, the more *important* the service will be; the framework will inject the service with the highest ranking of the available services. This way we can implement graceful degradation in an easy way. We simply deploy a fallback service with a lower ranking that will automatically take over when we deregister the higher ranked service. The service ranking property is an integer with a default value of `0`.

Service Registration and Deregistration Callbacks

In most cases, when we inject references to services, we just want to use the service. In some more advanced cases, it can be useful to execute some code whenever the service dependency becomes available or unavailable. We can do so in Apache Felix Dependency Manager by specifying callbacks in the activator. Callbacks are basically setter methods that are invoked on service (de)registration. Apache Felix Dependency Manager accepts different combinations of parameters in callback methods, which will be detected automatically.

First we will need to specify the callbacks in the activator. The method names are passed in as strings to the `setCallbacks` method:

Activator:

```
manager.add(createComponent()
    .setInterface(Object.class.getName(), null)
    .setImplementation(OtherComponent.class)
    .add(createServiceDependency()
        .setService(Greeter.class)
        .setCallbacks("serviceAdded", "serviceRemoved")));
```

Next we need to write callback methods in the component implementation. The following are several examples of callbacks using different argument types:

Simple callbacks:

```
public void serviceAdded(Greeter greeter) {
    System.out.println("Greeter added!");
}

public void serviceRemoved() {
    System.out.println("Goodbye greeter!");
}
```

Service reference:

```
public void serviceAdded(ServiceReference ref, Greeter greeter) {
    System.out.println("Greeter added with PID: " +
        ref.getProperty(Constants.SERVICE_PID));
}
```

```
    public void serviceRemoved(ServiceReference ref) {
        System.out.println("Goodbye service with PID: " +
            ref.getProperty(Constants.SERVICE_PID));
    }
```

Injecting Multiple Service Implementations and the Whiteboard Pattern

Besides injecting single services, it can also be useful to inject multiple service implementations. This is the basis for the *whiteboard design pattern*. The whiteboard pattern is a very clean way of implementing event listeners. The traditional pattern of event listeners is to make the event listeners implement an interface and register themselves to the event producer as listeners. A huge disadvantage of this pattern is the coupling between the event producer and listeners; listeners must register themselves to a specific instance of a producer, and producers must maintain a list of listeners. Especially in a dynamic environment like OSGi, this becomes very challenging because both producers and listeners can come and go during runtime.

The whiteboard pattern offers a cleaner way to deal with this concept. Instead of registering listeners directly to the producer, we use the service registry as a middle man. The event listeners are registered to the service registry as OSGi services. The event producer simply looks up all listeners from the registry. Instead of looking up services manually, we can of course use Apache Felix Dependency Manager to inject the list of listeners. Because the list of services can change any given moment, we use callback methods to be notified when a service is registered or deregistered.

The following example is a service with callbacks for Greeter services:

```
    private Map<String, Greeter> greeters = new ConcurrentHashMap<>();

    public void serviceAdded(ServiceReference ref, Greeter greeter) {
        String pid = ref.getProperty(Constants.SERVICE_PID));
        greeters.put(pid, greeter);

    }

    public void serviceRemoved(ServiceReference ref) {
        String pid = ref.getProperty(Constants.SERVICE_PID));
        greeters.remove(pid);
    }
```

Having a map of properties, we could iterate over all greeters and use them all to say hello:

```
    public void sayHello() {
        for (String pid : greeters.keySet()) {
            System.out.println(pid + " says " + greeters.get(pid).sayHello());
```

```
        }
    }
```

Registration of this service is the same as in the previous example: we simply configure the callback methods, and Apache Felix Dependency Manager takes care of the rest. Here is the `activator`:

```
manager.add(createComponent()
    .setInterface(Object.class.getName(), null)
    .setImplementation(OtherComponent.class)
    .add(createServiceDependency()
        .setService(Greeter.class)
        .setCallbacks("serviceAdded", "serviceRemoved")));
```

Besides the obvious example of event listeners, this pattern is often used in frameworks in OSGi. In a later chapter of the book, we will look at RESTful web services provided by Amdatu, for example. Amdatu picks up your classes and registers them as JAX-RS resources using this very same whiteboard pattern.

Lifecycle Callbacks

Although not necessary in many cases, it is possible to specify callbacks for component *start* and *stop* events. This is not the same as the `init` and `destroy` methods of a bundle activator. The bundle activator methods are invoked when the bundle is started and stopped. The Apache Felix Dependency Manager callbacks work on the component level; they are invoked when the component is registered and deregistered. This is only after the required dependencies of the service are available. There are four callback methods: `init`, `start`, `stop`, and `destroy`. The difference between `init` and `start` is that during `init`, it is still possible to add more dependencies to the component. The `start` method is only called after those dependencies became available as well. The difference between `stop` and `destroy` is that `stop` is called before services provided by the component are deregistered, while `destroy` is called after service deregistration.

By default Apache Felix Dependency Manager will look for void methods called `start`, `stop`, `init`, and `destroy`; you don't have to configure anything for this as you can see in the activator:

```
public class CallbackExample {

    public void init() {
        // A convenient place to add extra dependencies
        System.out.println("Init");
    }

    public void start() {
        System.out.println("Starting");
    }

    public void stop() {
```

```
        System.out.println("Stopping");
    }

    public void destroy() {
        System.out.println("Destroy");
    }
}

public class Activator extends DependencyActivatorBase{

    @Override
    public void init(BundleContext context, DependencyManager manager)
        throws Exception {
        manager.add(createComponent()
            .setInterface(Object.class.getName(), null)
            .setImplementation(CallbackExample.class));
    }

    @Override
    public void destroy(BundleContext context, DependencyManager manager)
        throws Exception {
    }
}
```

The example shows that there is no need to implement any interfaces to support call-backs. Apache Felix Dependency Manager works by convention instead. This has the (somewhat theoretical) benefit of not tying your code to Apache Felix Dependency Manager.

We can also override the callback method names:

```
manager.add(createComponent()
    .setInterface(Object.class.getName(), null)
    .setImplementation(CallbackExample.class)
    .setCallbacks("myInit", "myStart", "myStop", "myDestroy"));
```

Injecting BundleContext and DependencyManager

In some cases, we might need a reference to the BundleContext. The BundleContext gives us access to useful things like the bundle cache storage area and the bundle itself. It also gives us the ability to look up other bundles. We can simply add an instance variable of type BundleContext, and Apache Felix Dependency Manager will inject the BundleContext into this automatically:

```java
public class BundleContextExample {
    private volatile BundleContext context;

    public void myStart() {
        // Create a reference to a file in the bundle cache of this bundle
        File dataFile = context.getDataFile("mystorage.cer");

        // Get the bundle id
        long bundleId = context.getBundle().getBundleId();

        // List files and directories on the root of the bundle
        Enumeration entryPaths = context.getBundle().getEntryPaths("/");
        while (entryPaths.hasMoreElements()) {
            System.out.println(entryPaths.nextElement());
        }
    }
}
```

CHAPTER 4

Advanced OSGi

In this chapter, we will dive into some of the more advanced topics that you will need to know about when developing applications with OSGi, unleashing its full potential.

Semantic Versioning

In OSGi, package imports and exports are versioned. We discussed the syntax of version ranges before but did not delve into the details of how to version in the first place. The OSGi Alliance published a paper about *semantic versioning*, which describes a set of rules that define what version bumps are required for certain code changes. Adhering to these rules when releasing your bundles will help to detect backward compatibility problems when you, or users of your bundle, upgrade to newer versions. Semantic versioning makes it much easier to reason about versions. As with many things in OSGi, it's about finding problems early during development and deployment, instead of unexpected runtime behavior. Being able to safely depend on a version range as large as possible also increases decoupling. If a component works with a wide range of versions of another component, it's more loosely coupled than when it could only work with a very strict version.

In semantic versioning, there are four parts that make up a version: `major.minor. micro.qualifier`. The qualifier does not have much semantics; it can contain any string. The `major.minor.micro` format does have clear semantics:

Major
> API change that breaks consumers of the API

Minor
> API change that breaks providers of the API

Micro
> Changes that don't affect backward compatibility

So what exactly does it mean to break an API?

Provider and Consumer Types

When talking about API changes, we make a difference between *consumers* and *providers* of the API. A consumer of an interface uses, but doesn't implement, the interface. If we are using the `org.osgi.service.log.LogService` interface for logging in our code, we are a consumer of that interface. If we would implement our own logging implementation by implementing the `LogService` interface, we would become a provider of that interface.

Some interfaces are implemented by, at most, a few implementations but used by many. `LogService` is an example of this; there are only a handful of libraries that implement the `LogService` interface, but the interface is used everywhere code needs to log something. We call such interfaces *provider types*. Other interfaces are used the other way around: they are implemented many times but are only used by a handful of implementations. `javax.servlet.Filter` is an example of this; many servlet filters are created by developers, but they are only consumed by a handful of application servers. We call such interfaces *consumer types*.

A change to a consumer type typically affects much more code compared to breaking a provider type. When a method is added to a provider type like `LogService`, we only have to fix a handful of libraries that implement this interface. The endless list of consumers of the `LogService` are not affected; they will still compile. Adding a method to `javax.servlet.Filter` would be more problematic. Everyone who implemented a servlet filter would have to implement this method to compile to the new interface version!

When it comes to semantic versioning, the rules are different for provider and consumer types. The rules are described in Tables 4-1 and 4-2.

Table 4-1. Versioning rules for provider types

Change	Version affected
Add method	Minor
Remove method	Major
Change method signature	Major
Change method implementation (for classes)	Micro

Table 4-2. Versioning rules for consumer types

Change	Version affected
Add method	Major
Remove method	Major
Change method signature	Major
Change method implementation (for classes)	Micro

In BND, we can explicitly specify what type a class or interface is by using the annotations `@ProviderType` and `@ConsumerType`. These annotations are compile-time only and serve as metadata for the tooling. When these annotations are used, BND can make a better choice on what rules to apply during *baselining*, which is discussed below. If no `@ProviderType` or `@ConsumerType` is specified, BND assumes the worst case scenario, which is consumer type.

Baselining in Bndtools

The semantic versioning rules are not very complex. It's easy to forget to bump versions during development, however, and tracking back the correct version bump at release time is often difficult if there were many changes by multiple developers. Bumping the version should also be done as soon as possible during development. If we bump a version, and some other bundles need to update their package imports, we want to see this right away at development time.

Bndtools has built-in support for doing this automatically. When the first version of a bundle is released in Bndtools, it's stored in a *release repository* (in the *cnf* project by default). When we then start making changes to code, Bndtools will immediately tell us that version bumps of both export packages and the bundle are required. It will also tell us what type of bump is required (major/minor/micro).

Bndtools does this by comparing the released bundle (the baseline) with the just built bundle, and applies the semantic versioning rules described earlier. After a code change, we will immediately see errors in our project, whose descriptions will tell us what to do. After bumping the version, we can keep making changes without any more errors until we apply a change that requires a higher version bump. For example, after bumping the minor version, we can make other minor changes to that package without bumping the version again.

After releasing the bundle, Bndtools will start baselining against the newly released bundle.

Semantic Bundle Versioning

So far we have been talking about semantic versioning on exported packages. This is what's most important, because we only import packages, never bundles. Technically it is good enough to make any change to the bundle version when something inside the bundle is changed. Applying semantic versioning is a nice bonus and communicates to users what to expect from a backward-compatibility perspective.

The bundle version should be an aggregation of the export package version bumps. If we have at least one major bump in one of the exported packages, the bundle version should have a major bump as well. If we only have minor bumps in the exported packages, the bundle version is bumped a minor version as well.

Integration Testing

Unit testing your code is very easy when OSGi is applied in the correct way. Most of the code doesn't depend on framework classes, and working with services automatically forces you to write code to interfaces instead of implementation classes, which is one of the most important steps toward (unit) testability. Basically there is nothing that makes it difficult to write unit tests when using OSGi, and you can use your favorite unit testing and mocking framework to do so.

For most code that we write, unit testing is not sufficient. How would you test queries in a data access service? Or how would you test service dynamics or configuration? Mocking the database and the framework would make it impossible to test the real important parts of code. For these situations, you need to run tests in a more realistic environment. In an OSGi environment, that means running tests in an OSGi framework. Because an OSGi framework is easy to bootstrap, this is easy to accomplish, and there are several frameworks to make this task even more trivial. Because we focus on the use of Bndtools in this book, we will also use the integration testing features from BND. BND integration tests can run *headless* on a CI server as well.

Writing Integration Tests

Integration tests in Bndtools are written as normal JUnit tests. While running them, they will be packaged as a bundle and installed in a real OSGi framework. The unit test code is basically just code in a bundle like all other code, but BND reports test results the same way as normal JUnit tests. Besides simply writing the test code, we also have to configure the runtime with just the set of bundles that we need to execute the test. Let's walk through this for a simple test case before we look into more advanced scenarios.

It is a best practice to create a separate Bndtools project for each set of integration tests that test one small part of the system (an OSGi service in most cases). This makes it easier to configure a small runtime for each set of integration tests. In many cases, we create one test project per Bndtools project; if we have an `org.example.demo` project, we will also create `org.example.demo.test`.

We will create an integration test for the `Greeter` service we created in the previous chapter. If you didn't follow the hands-on part, don't worry, the example will be easy to understand nevertheless.

Start by creating a new Bndtools project, and choose the Integration Test project template wizard. A template test class is already created. As you can see, the test class extends `TestCase` just like any plain JUnit test. However, the next line is more interesting:

```
private final BundleContext context = FrameworkUtil
    .getBundle(this.getClass()).getBundleContext();
```

The `FrameworkUtil` class gives access to the OSGi framework, in this case to retrieve the `BundleContext`. This obviously only works when the code runs in a real OSGi framework. More than that, the `Bundle` for the current class (the test class itself) is looked up. This means that the test itself is running in a bundle as well.

Having the `BundleContext`, we can do anything we like in the OSGi framework. In many cases, we will use the `BundleContext` in an integration test to look up the service that we are testing. The following is a simplified example that ignores the possibility of the service not being available:

```
public class GreeterTest extends TestCase {

    private final BundleContext context =
        FrameworkUtil.getBundle(this.getClass()).getBundleContext();

    public void testGreeter() throws Exception {
        ServiceReference<Greeter> serviceReference =
            context.getServiceReference(Greeter.class);
        Greeter greeter = context.getService(serviceReference);
        String greeting = greeter.sayHello();
        assertEquals("Hello modular world", greeting);
    }
}
```

Note that this code is clearly wrong! As with any code that uses the low-level services API, you should be doing all the `null` checks and deal with the possibility that a service was not registered yet. This becomes very tricky when the test involves multiple services, which is the case in most nontrivial examples. That's a lot of work for a test! Instead of doing all that hard work ourselves, we could use the service tracker specification, or even better, Apache Felix Dependency Manager in the tests. The following example uses Apache Felix Dependency Manager to make the test class itself a component and wait until its dependencies (the services we want to test) are injected:

```
public class GreeterTest extends TestCase {
    private final BundleContext context = FrameworkUtil.getBundle(
```

```
            this.getClass()).getBundleContext();
    private CountDownLatch latch;
    private Greeter greeter;

    public void start() throws InterruptedException {
        latch.countDown();
    }

    @Override
    protected void setUp()  {
        latch = new CountDownLatch(1);

        DependencyManager dm = new DependencyManager(context);
        dm.add(dm.createComponent()
            .setImplementation(this)
            .add(dm.createServiceDependency()
                .setService(Greeter.class)));

        try {
            latch.await(10, TimeUnit.SECONDS);
        } catch (InterruptedException e) {
            fail("Service dependencies were not injected.");
        }
    }

    public void testGreeter() throws Exception {
        System.out.println(greeter.sayHello());
    }
}
```

Amdatu offers a test base class that your test class can extend to make testing even easier. The implementation of the base class is not listed here because it is quite large, but an example of the actual test class follows. The base class is based on Apache Felix Dependency Manager and automatically injects an instance of the service being tested in the test class. You can also configure managed services and declaratively inject other services into the test:

```
import org.amdatu.mongo.MongoDBService;
// Other imports omitted for brevity

public class MongoProductServiceTest extends
    BaseOSGiServiceTest<ProductService> {
    private volatile MongoDBService mongoDBService;
    private DBCollection collection;

    public MongoProductServiceTest() {
        super(ProductService.class);
    }

    @Override
    public void setUp() throws Exception {
```

```java
    // Configure a Managed Service
    Properties properties = new Properties();
    properties.put("dbName", "webshoptests");
    configureFactory("org.amdatu.mongo", properties);

    // Inject more service dependencies into the test
    addServiceDependencies(MongoDBService.class);

    // Wait for services to become available (timeout after 10 seconds)
    super.setUp();

    // Optionally do some additional setup using the injected services
    collection = mongoDBService.getDB().getCollection("products");
    collection.remove(new BasicDBObject());
}

// The actual tests, using real services
public void testListCategories() {
    collection.save(new BasicDBObject("category", "books"));
    collection.save(new BasicDBObject("category", "books"));
    collection.save(new BasicDBObject("category", "games"));

    List<String> categories = instance.listCategories();
    assertEquals(2, categories.size());
}

}
```

Running Integration Tests

The test code that we have seen is clearly not a normal unit test; it uses the Bundle Context and service registry. To run this test, we need to configure a runtime. Open the *bnd.bnd* file of the test project and open the Run tab. Here we can configure our test runtime just like we configure a normal runtime. Add the bundle that contains the Greeter service to the Run Requirements and click Resolve. Now right-click the bnd file and choose Run as → OSGi JUnit test. In the IDE you will just see JUnit test results, but under the covers, the following things happen:

- The test bundle is packaged.
- The OSGi framework is started.
- Bundles on the Run Bundles list will be installed.
- Test bundles will be looked up.
- Tests are executed (within the runtime).

If you add an OSGi shell (such as the Gogo shell) to the Run Requirements and set a breakpoint in your test, you can actually just take a look at the running runtime like it is a normal OSGi application (in fact, it is). You might be wondering how your tests are found and executed in the runtime. This is caused by an additional header in the *bnd.bnd* file. Take a look at the source of the file, and you will find the following header:

```
Test-Cases: ${classes;CONCRETE;EXTENDS;junit.framework.TestCase}
```

This is another example of the whiteboard pattern. The test framework will look for bundles with this header. Also note that this header is a BND macro, it will be processed at bundle build time. Take a look at the generated bundle to see the result.

Running integration tests from the IDE is easy. But what about running a headless build on a continuous integration server? Bndtools automatically creates ANT build files for each project that you create. The ANT build already includes support for integration testing. Open a terminal in your project folder and simply run ANT:

```
ant test
```

This means that every Bndtools project can be built and tested on a continuous integration server out of the box.

Configuring Services

Configuration is part of almost every production application. We probably don't have to explain why it's a bad idea to hardcode configuration settings such as database passwords. In an OSGi context, configuration is mostly about configuring services because services are the core of the programming model. We could very well have a service responsible for database access, and that service should be configured with the correct database configuration.

In a modular world, configuration becomes even more important for another reason. Modules can very well become reusable modules, usable in many different systems. It's not hard to imagine how a flexible, configurable component is more reusable. When building reusable modules, it's important that the way those modules are configured is flexible as well. In many non-OSGi applications, you will find configuration in several different forms: some libraries need property files, (proprietary) XML, system properties, a Java API, and so on. It would be a lot simpler if all configuration could be passed to the system in a single way. OSGi Compendium has a specification for this: Configuration Admin.

Configuration Admin specifies a Java API to configure services, and interfaces for configurable services. Configuration Admin is more or less a middle man for configuration. Instead of passing configuration directly to your code, configuration is passed to Configuration Admin using the service.pid of the service that needs to be configured. The service.pid is the *persistent* ID of a service; in contrast to the service.id, it is known even before the service is available. Configuration Admin will then configure services in a standardized way using this configuration. By introducing this middle man, we decouple the way configuration is passed to the system from the actual configuration of services. Using extensions, it is possible to pass configuration to Configuration Admin using the Java API directly, using MetaType (an XML standard for configuration), properties files, or even the web console. Figure 4-1 shows the decoupling between configuration and the configured services.

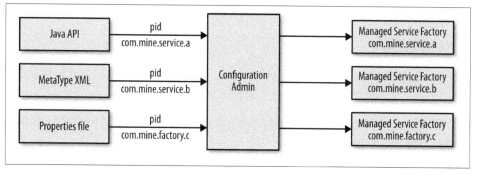

Figure 4-1. Configuration Admin

Managed Services

The simplest and most common form of configurable services are `ManagedServices`. A `ManagedService` is a single service that accepts configuration. A `ManagedService` is a normal service, with the addition of implementing the `ManagedService` interface. This interface has one method:

```
void updated(Dictionary properties) throws ConfigurationException
```

The updated method receives a `Dictionary` of properties and is called by Configuration Admin. In many cases, the updated method is used to simply set instance variables of the service that contain the configurable properties. Make sure the updated method is thread-safe. It might be called by a Configuration Admin thread while the service is being called by another thread.

A simple example of a Managed Service is the following Greeter. The Greeter can be configured with a message that will be used when the `hello` method is invoked:

```
public class ConfigurableGreeter implements Greeter, ManagedService {
    private final String DEFAULT_MESSAGE = "Default greeting";
    private String message = DEFAULT_MESSAGE;

    @Override
    public void updated(Dictionary properties) throws ConfigurationException {
        if (properties != null) {
            Object messageProperty = properties.get("message");
            if (messageProperty != null) {
                message = (String) messageProperty;
            } else {
                // Invalid configuration, throw exception.
```

```
                    throw new ConfigurationException("message",
                        "Required property message missing");
                }
            } else {
                // Configuration deleted, fall back to defaults.
                message = DEFAULT_MESSAGE;
            }
        }

        @Override
        public void sayHello() {
            System.out.println(message);
        }
    }
```

Note that you cannot use any injected service dependencies from the updated method because they might not be injected yet.

The service is implementing both its own service interface `Greeter` and the `Managed Service` interface. Make sure you always check the `Dictionary` for `null` because Configuration Admin will call the updated method with `null` if no configuration is available yet. Even if you require configuration to always be present, there might be a race condition where the Managed Service is registered before the configuration. This service also works when no configuration is available. The updated method should throw a `ConfigurationException` when the configuration is invalid, e.g., when the `message` property is missing.

In some cases configuration is required; see "Required Configuration" on page 56 for that.

Before we can start using a Managed Service, it needs be registered as a service like any other service. Because an OSGi service is only registered using a single interface, we will have to do something extra. We will register the service twice, once as a `Greeter` and once as a `ManagedService`. The Managed Service also requires the service property `service.pid` to be set.

Using Apache Felix Dependency Manager, the activator could be the following:

```
    public class Activator extends DependencyActivatorBase {

        @Override
        public void init(BundleContext context, DependencyManager manager)
            throws Exception {

            Properties properties = new Properties();
            properties.setProperty(Constants.SERVICE_PID,
                "example.managedservice.greeter");

            manager.add(createComponent()
                .setInterface(new String[] {Greeter.class.getName(),
```

```
            ManagedService.class.getName()}, properties)
        .setImplementation(ConfigurableGreeter.class));
    }

    @Override
    public void destroy(BundleContext context, DependencyManager manager)
        throws Exception {
    }
}
```

Configuring a Managed Service

Now that we have seen how to create and publish Managed Services, we need to know how to configure those services. Configuration Admin comes with a simple Java API to do so. Remember that you will not use this API in most situations, but will use external files such as MetaType XML for this. Especially during integration testing, it is convenient to use the Configuration Admin API directly. Let's look at the API first:

```
// ConfigAdmin is just another service that you can inject or lookup
ConfigurationAdmin configAdmin;

Configuration configuration =
configAdmin.getConfiguration("example.managedservice.greeter", null);

Properties properties = new Properties();
properties.setProperty("message","Hello modular world!");
configuration.update(properties);
```

Using this API, we can write an integration test for the configurable Greeter. The example is based on the Amdatu test base class again like we have seen in "Writing Integration Tests". First we test if the Greeter service works correctly without configuration. After that, we use the Configuration Admin service to create a new configuration for the Greeter service. After setting the configuration, the test waits for a second for Configuration Admin to process the configuration update before we test the now configured Greeter service again:

```
public class GreeterTest extends BaseOSGiServiceTest<Greeter> {
    private volatile ConfigurationAdmin configurationAdmin;

    public GreeterTest() {
        super(Greeter.class);
    }

    @Override
    public void setUp() throws Exception {
        addServiceDependencies(ConfigurationAdmin.class);
        super.setUp();
    }

    public void testConfiguredGreeter() throws Exception {
```

```
        assertEquals("Default greeting", instance.sayHello());

        Configuration configuration = configurationAdmin
            .getConfiguration("example.managedservice.greeter", null);

        Properties properties = new Properties();
        properties.setProperty("message", "Hello modular world!");
        configuration.update(properties);
        TimeUnit.SECONDS.sleep(1);

        assertEquals("Hello modular world!", instance.sayHello());
    }
}
```

Using the Amdatu test base class, we can even further simplify the test. The base class has helper methods to configure services. These helper methods basically do the same as what we did in the previous example:

```
public class GreeterTest extends BaseOSGiServiceTest<Greeter> {

    public GreeterTest() {
        super(Greeter.class);
    }

    public void testConfiguredGreeter() throws Exception {
        assertEquals("Default greeting", instance.sayHello());

        configure("example.managedservice.greeter", "message",
            "Configured greeting");

        TimeUnit.SECONDS.sleep(1);

        assertEquals("Configured greeting", instance.sayHello());
    }
}
```

Required Configuration

In the example in the previous section, the configuration is not required to be set for the service to become available. However, in some cases, configuration is required for a service to function correctly. To stick with the example of a service that does database access, without database connection information, the service can't do much useful work. Of course we could throw exceptions when this happens, but this makes using the service much more cumbersome. It's much more convenient to have a service that only becomes available when it is configured correctly. A service that has a required dependency on configuration.

Apache Felix Dependency Manager can do this with a single line of code while creating a component. Take the following modified Activator for the Greeter service as an example:

```
public class Activator extends DependencyActivatorBase {

    @Override
    public void init(BundleContext context, DependencyManager manager)
        throws Exception {

        manager.add(createComponent()
            .setInterface(Greeter.class.getName(), null)
            .setImplementation(ConfigurableGreeter.class)
            .add(createConfigurationDependency()
                .setPid("example.managedservice.greeter")));
    }

    @Override
    public void destroy(BundleContext context, DependencyManager manager)
        throws Exception {
    }
}
```

As you can see, we only register one component now, the Greeter itself, and not a separate Managed Service. By adding a configuration dependency, Apache Felix Dependency Manager will take care of setting this up.

When we want to test this using the Amdatu test base class, we have to make sure to configure the service before calling the super.setUp method. The setUp method waits for services to become available, so our test will not even start until the configuration is available:

```
public class GreeterTest extends BaseOSGiServiceTest<Greeter> {

    public GreeterTest() {
        super(Greeter.class);
    }

    @Override
    public void setUp() throws Exception {
        configure("example.managedservice.greeter", "message",
            "Hello modular world!");
        super.setUp();
    }

    public void testConfiguredGreeter() throws Exception {
        assertEquals("Hello modular world!", instance.sayHello());
    }
}
```

Managed Service Factories

For some services, it is required to have multiple instances of the service. Again, if we take a generic database access service as an example, we could have the requirement of working with multiple databases in a single application. For each configured database, we should have a new instance of the service. In "Service Properties" on page 39, we have seen how we can distinguish service instances with the same interface using service properties.

Managed Service Factories can be used to implement this use case. A Managed Service Factory is similar to a Managed Service in the way that it can be configured using Configuration Admin. However, instead of configuring itself, it creates and configures a new service instance every time the factory receives new configuration.

A Managed Service Factory must implement the `ManagedServiceFactory` interface from OSGi Compendium. The interface has three methods:

```
String getName()
void updated(String pid, Dictionary properties) throws ConfigurationException
void deleted(String pid)
```

The `getName` method only gives a descriptive name of the factory and has no technical consequences. The `updated` and `deleted` methods are more interesting. The `updated` method is invoked when configuration is added or updated. The `updated` method receives a PID, which is the unique ID of the configuration object representing this configuration. If it is a new PID, the Managed Service Factory can create a new service instance and register it to the service registry. The service created by the Managed Service Factory should not be a Managed Service itself, because it will only be reconfigured using the Managed Service Factory.

When the `updated` method is called with a PID that is already known to the Managed Service Factory, configuration for an existing configuration object is being updated. In most cases, this should result in updating an existing service. In case of an error in the configuration (e.g., a missing required property), the Managed Service Factory should throw a `ConfigurationException`. When configuration is removed from Configuration Admin for a given PID, the `deleted` method will be invoked, and from this method, the services registered for this PID should be deregistered.

As you can see, it is important for a Managed Service Factory to keep track of the PIDs known by the Managed Service Factory. You will have to write code for this yourself, as you will see in the example.

Let's take a look at a revised Greeter, where we can have multiple Greeters with different messages. The Greeter implementation itself can now be simpler because we don't need to implement the `ManagedService` interface:

```
public class GreeterImpl implements Greeter{
    private volatile String message;

    @Override
    public String sayHello() {
        return message;
    }
```

```
    public void setMessage(String message) {
        this.message = message;
    }
}
```

The Managed Service Factory requires a little bit more code. The Managed Service Factory in this example creates and registers new Greeter services. With this example, there can be multiple greeters, recognizable by service properties. Take a look at the following example before we will walk through it step by step:

```
public class GreeterFactory implements ManagedServiceFactory {
    private volatile DependencyManager dependencyManager;
    private final Map<String, Component> components = new ConcurrentHashMap<>();

    @Override
    public String getName() {
        return "Greeter Factory";
    }

    @Override
    public void updated(String pid, Dictionary properties)
        throws ConfigurationException {
        String message = (String) properties.get("message");

        if (message == null) {
            throw new ConfigurationException("message",
                "Required property 'message' missing");
        }

        GreeterImpl greeter;
        Component greeterComponent = null;

        synchronized (components) {
            if (components.containsKey(pid)) {
                greeter = (GreeterImpl) components.get(pid).getService();
            } else {
                String type = (String) properties.get("type");

                if (type == null) {
                    throw new ConfigurationException("message",
                        "Required property 'type' missing");
                }

                greeter = new GreeterImpl();
                greeterComponent = dependencyManager.createComponent()
                    .setInterface(Greeter.class.getName(), properties)
                    .setImplementation(greeter);
                components.put(pid, greeterComponent);
            }
        }
    }
```

```
        // Calling services from a synchronized block can lead to deadlocks,
        // so Dependency Manager must be called outside.
        if(greeterComponent != null) {
            dependencyManager.add(greeterComponent);
        }
    }

    greeter.setMessage(message);
}

@Override
public void deleted(String pid) {
    Component component = null;
    synchronized (components) {
        component = components.remove(pid);
    }

    // Calling services from a synchronized block can lead to deadlocks,
    // so Dependency Manager must be called outside.
    if(component != null) {
        dependencyManager.remove(component);
    }
}
}
```

To make service registration easy, we are using Apache Felix Dependency Manager in the Managed Service Factory. A DependencyManager object is injected by Apache Felix Dependency Manager into the dependencyManager field. Apache Felix Dependency Manager does this automatically if it finds a field of type DependencyManager; you do not have to declare this explicitly. This factory implementation also keeps map of strings (the PIDs) and the Apache Felix Dependency Manager component instances. This housekeeping is required because we have to keep track of which PIDs we know about for update and delete purposes. Because the factory can create multiple service instances, it would be useful to add some service properties to the services so that we know the difference between the services created. For this we use the configuration property type, which is added to the service that gets registered. Note that this implementation doesn't support changes to the type property after initial registration to keep the example concise.

In the updated method, we first do some input validation on the message configuration property. If the message property is not available, we throw a ConfigurationException.

Next we have to decide if an existing Greeter service should be updated with a new message, or if we have to create a new service instance. For this, we look up the PID in the map of registered services. If we have to create a new service, we use Apache Felix Dependency Manager to create a new component. The service is just a Greeter service, there is nothing special about this instance. However, we do add the type service property.

Note that the PID passed to both the `updated` and `deleted` methods is the PID of a `Configuration` object. This is not the same and not related to the PID of the actual service that we create.

At the bottom of the `updated` method, we finally do the actual configuration of the service by calling the `setMessage` method.

When a `Configuration` object is deleted, the `deleted` method will be invoked with the PID of the deleted `Configuration` object. We have to take care of deregistration of the service.

Implementing a Managed Service Factory is considerably more work than a Managed Service. However, it gives a lot of freedom on what happens when configuration is found. If you want to take a look at a more real-world example, the open source Amdatu Mongo project is a nice example. We will use this in a later chapter to create MongoDB services, but it is interesting to look at the code to see how a slightly more complex Managed Service Factory would look, although the mechanisms remain the same.

MetaType

The OSGi Compendium contains another configuration-related specification: *Meta-Type*. The goal of MetaType is to provide metadata about configuration. Based on this, metadata user interfaces can be generated for your configuration. For example, this can be used with Apache Felix Web Console. Later in this book, we will discuss Apache Felix Web Console in more detail, but it is a browser-based management environment for OSGi applications. It provides a shell, bundle and service overview, configuration panels, etc., all in a browser. When MetaType is provided with your Managed Service, Web Console will automatically provide a user interface to edit the configuration properties.

Using MetaType is very easy; just provide an extra XML file within your bundle. The following example could be a MetaType file for the Greeter Managed Service:

```
<?xml version="1.0" encoding="UTF-8"?>
<metatype:MetaData xmlns:metatype="http://www.osgi.org/xmlns/metatype/v1.0.0">
    <OCD description="Greeter Service" name="Greeter"
        id="example.managedservice.greeter">
        <AD name="Greeting message" id="example.managedservice.greeter.message"
            required="true" type="String" default="Hello"/>
    </OCD>

    <Designate pid="example.managedservice.greeter">
        <Object ocdref="example.managedservice.greeter"/>
    </Designate>
</metatype:MetaData>
```

There are three parts in this file:

AD *(Attribute Definition)*
> Describes an configuration property and its type.

OCD *(Object Class Definition)*
> Grouping of a set of attributes; provides a description for the set of attributes.

Designate
> Connects MetaType to a Managed Service or Managed Service Factory PID. Note that the PID is independent of the package and class name of the Managed Service.

A MetaType file must be provided at the following location in a bundle:

```
OSGI-INF/metatype/metatype.xml
```

In Bndtools, you can do so by adding an *include resource* definition in your bnd file. Assuming that you created the MetaType file in a subdirectory of your Bndtools project *metatype/metatype.xml*, the following line in the bnd file would add it to the bundle:

```
-includeresource: OSGI-INF/metatype=metatype
```

If you now add Apache Felix Web Console to your run requirements, you can access it on *http://localhost:8080/system/console*. Your configuration properties specified in MetaType should now show up (and be editable) on the configuration tab.

Providing Configuration

We have seen the Configuration Admin Java API and the Metatype XML format. We did not discuss how to provide configuration to a real application yet. Because anyone can implement some kind of extension on top of Configuration Admin, the possibilities are endless. We will discuss some common ways:

- Apache Felix File Install
- Apache ACE

A common way to provide externalized configuration to an application is to use Apache Felix File Install. When the File Install bundle is installed, it will watch a directory for bundles and configuration files. Bundles found in the directory will be installed, and configuration is passed to Configuration Admin. Apache Felix File Install uses simple property files for configuration. The name of the file should be the configuration's PID, and have the extension *.cfg*. For a Managed Service with PID *com.example.someservice*, you would create a file *com.example.someservice.cfg*. The contents of the file should be simple key/value pairs. By default, Apache Felix File Install watches a directory `load` and can be configured to watch other directories using the `felix.fileinstall.dir` system property.

Because a Managed Service Factory can receive multiple configurations, Apache Felix File Install uses a slightly different filenaming schema. Configuration files should be postfixed -*somename*, e.g., *com.example.someservice.factory-myexample.cfg*.

When configuration managed by Apache Felix File Install is modified, it will write the modified configuration back to the property file.

In more advanced (e.g., in the cloud) deployment scenarios, Apache Felix File Install doesn't suffice. We will discuss Apache ACE as a provisioning solution later on in this book. Apache ACE can be used to provision configuration as well, with some more advanced options, such as postprocessing the configuration files.

Log Service

OSGi has a standard API available for logging. The specification consists of two services: one for writing log messages and one for reading. The API for writing log messages is similar to other logging frameworks. There are several implementations of the LogSer vice that can be used directly, some of them offering features such as Gogo and Web Console integration.

Logging in a modular application is not any different from logging in a nonmodular application. The same rules about what to log and what not to log apply. In a dynamic services environment, there are some more events that we might want to log; for example, services coming and going.

From an application developer perspective, you will mostly only use the API for writing log messages. Reading log messages is handled by implementations. The LogService API has only four methods:

```
// Log a message at the given level
log(int, String)

// Log a message with an exception at the given level
log(int, String, Throwable)

// Log a message for a specific service
log(ServiceReference, int, String)

// Log a message with an exception for a specific service
log(ServiceReference, int, String, Throwable)
```

The log levels are defined by LogService as well:

- LogService.LOG_DEBUG
- LogService.LOG_INFO

- LogService.LOG_WARNING
- LogService.LOG_ERROR

Installing and Using the LogService

Download Apache Felix Log and add it to the run configuration of your project. The LogService is an OSGi service, so we can use Apache Felix Dependency Manager (or another dependency injection framework) to inject the LogService in our code. In general, a dependency on LogService should be optional; most code can still execute without any problem without the availability of logging.

The following code shows an Apache Felix Dependency Manager activator example:

```
dependencyManager.add(createComponent()
    .setImplementation(MyComponent.class)
    .add(createServiceDependency()
        .setService(LogService.class)));
```

And the component that uses the LogService:

```
public class MyComponent {
    private volatile LogService logService;

    public void doSomething() {
        logService.log(LogService.LOG_INFO, "Log example");
    }
}
```

Assuming that you are using the Gogo shell, you can now retrieve log messages using the shell:

```
g! log 1 info
```

Logging Performance

In any system, it is important to log messages at the correct logging level. Not only would it clutter the logs if less important messages are logged at a high logging level, but it might also impact performance. Debug level messages are not very useful in production, but logging thousands of them can have a very negative effect on performance.

Although log levels can be specified in most Log Service implementations, the OSGi Log Service specification unfortunately contains a section that makes all log messages affect performance, even log messages at levels that are not further processed by the logging implementation. The specification states that all log messages should be forwarded to Event Admin, in case any listener is interested. Even if there are no listeners for these log messages, sending them to Event Admin still costs CPU cycles.

Extender Pattern

It is very common to have extensions (or plug-ins) in an OSGi application. We have already discussed the whiteboard pattern, which is the most common way to deal with extensions. The whiteboard pattern is based on services; an extension would register a new service of a given interface so that the service will be picked up by the mechanism that manages the extensions.

The whiteboard pattern is great because it is quite simple; you register extensions as services and service trackers to pick up those services. In some rare cases, the need to register services might feel like a burden. This might be the case when you have bundles with no code besides an activator that registers a service. This is a sign that the Extender pattern might be a better solution. A real-life example of this is bundles with only web resources (HTML files, etc.) in them. Those web resources should be exposed on a certain context path.

The Extender pattern listens for bundle registrations. For each bundle registration, it then checks if the extender applies to that specific bundle. If the bundle should be extended, it then uses that bundle to do so, for example registering its web resources to a servlet. The decision about whether the bundle does or does not apply for extension is mostly based on some kind of marker. Although any kind of marker can be used, it is most common to use a manifest header for this. By using a marker, we can easily discard bundles that don't apply for extension without scanning the bundle contents.

Let's create a trivial implementation of an extender that exposes web resources using a servlet. We didn't discuss servlets or the HTTP Service yet, but that shouldn't matter too much for this example. If you want to know more about the HTTP Service, you can skip forward to Chapter 8. Also note that you should not use this example in production. If you want to have a production ready implementation of this example, take a look at the Amdatu Resource Handler.

Using this example extender, we should be able to create bundles containing only web resources such as HTML, CSS, and JavaScript files. The extender should make these files accessible on the Web on a defined context path. We could of course simply do this with a servlet in each of those web resource bundles, but this would lead to duplicate code. Instead we want to write the registration code only once (in the extender) and provide plain resource bundles.

First we define an example resource bundle:

```
-META-INF
  -MANIFEST.MF
-static
  -index.html
  -css
    -style.css
```

In the manifest, we add one extra header:

```
X-WebResource: /myweb
```

Note that this header is just an example for our extender; this is by no means a standardized header. First of all, this header will be used as a marker to tell the extender that this is a bundle that should be extended. Second, it provides the path within the bundle that contains the web resources.

We now create an activator with a bundle dependency. A bundle dependency creates a callback to bundles changing states. Optionally a filter can be provided to only match bundles with specific headers in their manifest. This is exactly what we will use to only pickup bundles with the X-WebResource header. Besides the filter, a state mask can be specified. In most cases, we are only interested in ACTIVE bundles because the extension should be removed when the bundle is stopped:

```
public class Activator extends DependencyActivatorBase {
    @Override
    public void init(BundleContext context, DependencyManager manager)
        throws Exception {
        manager.add(createComponent()
            .setInterface(Object.class.getName(), null)
            .setImplementation(WebResourceHandler.class)
            .add(createBundleDependency()
                .setFilter("(X-WebResource=*)")
                .setCallbacks("bundleAdded", "bundleRemoved")
                .setStateMask(Bundle.ACTIVE)));
    }

    @Override
    public void destroy(BundleContext context, DependencyManager manager)
        throws Exception {
    }
}
```

The WebResourceHandler component has bundle add and remove callbacks. The state mask only matches active bundles. The WebResourceHandler will register a new component (a servlet) to the DependencyManager for each bundle found. Because the components created are part of the extender bundle instead of the resource bundles, it is important to also take care of deregistration of the components. When a resource bundle is stopped, its servlet should be deregistered as well:

```
public class WebResourceHandler {
    private volatile DependencyManager dm;
    private final Map<Long, Component> components = new ConcurrentHashMap<>();

    public void bundleAdded(Bundle bundle) {
        System.out.println("Resource Bundle found: " +
            bundle.getSymbolicName() +
            " with resources: " +
            bundle.getHeaders().get("X-WebResource"));
```

```
        ResourceServlet servlet = new ResourceServlet(bundle);

        Properties properties = new Properties();
        properties.put("alias", bundle.getHeaders().get("X-WebResource"));
        Component component = dm.createComponent()
            .setInterface(Servlet.class.getName(), properties)
            .setImplementation(servlet);
        components.put(bundle.getBundleId(), component);
        dm.add(component);
    }

    public void bundleRemoved(Bundle bundle) {
        System.out.println("Bundle removed: " + bundle.getSymbolicName());
        Component component = components.get(bundle.getBundleId());
        dm.remove(component);
        components.remove(bundle.getBundleId());
    }
}
```

The DependencyManager instance is injected by DependencyManager itself (because WebResourceHandler is a component as well). To be able to deregister components when their bundles are stopped, we keep a Map of bundleId and Component to track the created components.

When a new resource bundle is found, we read the X-WebResource header from the bundle. With that we register a new servlet on the alias of the X-WebResource value. This kind of servlet registration requires Apache Felix Whiteboard, as discussed in "Injecting Multiple Service Implementations and the Whiteboard Pattern" on page 41.

The servlet itself is very simple. On a GET request, we simply look up the resource from the bundle and return it back to the client. This example is not necessarily the most efficient way of streaming the resources, and should just be used as an example of an extender:

```
public class ResourceServlet extends HttpServlet{
    private final Bundle bundle;

    public ResourceServlet(Bundle bundle) {
        this.bundle = bundle;
    }

    @Override
    protected void doGet(HttpServletRequest req, HttpServletResponse resp)
        throws ServletException, IOException {
        String reqPath = req.getPathInfo();
        Object resourcesPath = bundle.getHeaders().get("X-WebResource");
        URL resource = bundle.getResource(resourcesPath + reqPath);
        try(InputStream inputStream = resource.openStream()) {
            // Use Apache Commons IO to copy the inputstream to output
            IOUtils.copy(inputStream, resp.getOutputStream());
```

```
        }
    }
}
```

Event Admin

Event Admin is an intra-bundle event publisher and subscriber model. You can compare this to other messaging systems such as JMS. Event Admin routes events within an OSGi framework over multiple bundles. This allows intra-bundle messaging without setting up interfaces and services to do so, which offers complete decoupling between event publishers and subscribers. The event publisher and subscriber pattern is specially convenient when many fine-grained events are used.

An example of Event Admin usage is the framework itself. Events are sent for framework events such as starting and stopping bundles.

In general, an event listener is only interested in specific types of events; for example, an event listener that handles new orders should not receive framework events. To facilitate this, Event Admin works with topics. A topic represents the type of event. Events are sent to specific topics, and listeners can choose to listen to only specific topics.

A topic name is a hierarchical namespace where each level is separated by a /. For example: `org/example/products/added`. The `EventAdmin` implementation can use this hierarchy for efficient filtering.

Messages can be sent either synchronously (using the `EventAdmin.sendEvent` method) or asynchronously (using the `EventAdmin.postEvent` method).

Using Event Admin

One of the available Event Admin implementations comes from Apache Felix. As usual, the bundle can be found on the Apache Felix website or in the Amdatu dependencies repository.

Add the Apache Felix `EventAdmin` bundle to your run configuration, and you're ready to send and receive events.

To send events, we need a reference to the `EventAdmin` service:

```
public class SenderExample {
    private volatile EventAdmin eventAdmin;

    public void start() {
        Map<String, Object> greeting = new HashMap<>();
        greeting.put("message", "Modular greetings");
        greeting.put("from", "the authors");

        // Send asynchronous message
```

```
        eventAdmin.sendEvent(new Event("examples/events/greetings", greeting));

        // Send asynchronous message
        eventAdmin.postEvent(new Event("examples/events/greetings", greeting));
    }
}
```

The example shows that the sendEvent and postEvent methods accept a type org.osgi.service.event.Event. The event type is created with a string that represents the topic name and a map containing the event properties. The event properties map can contain any type as values, but there are some limitations. Custom types are supported, but only when events are send within the OSGi framework because no serialization is required then. Some EventAdmin implementations support sending events to native (e.g., C/C++) applications. A native implementation must support strings, the primitive Java types, and single dimensional arrays. Other types might be supported, but this is not required.

If you use custom event types, you should make those types available for other bundles by exporting them; they wouldn't be usable by any other bundles otherwise. You can argue that introducing special event types creates some coupling between an event provider and consumer; this is a trade-off.

Event properties and their values should, as a best practice, be immutable. Mutable event types could potentially be modified by event listeners, and subsequent listeners would see the modified data.

Listening for events is easy as well. You need to register an OSGi service using interface org.osgi.service.event.EventHandler. EventAdmin will pick up this service whiteboard style; no explicit registration is required. The service should be registered with a service property EventConstants.EVENT_TOPIC that specifies the topic name to listen to:

```
public class ReceiverExample implements EventHandler{
    @Override
    public void handleEvent(Event event) {
        String message = (String)event.getProperty("message");
        String from = (String)event.getProperty("from");

        System.out.println("Message received from " + from + ": " + message);
    }
}

public class Activator extends DependencyActivatorBase{
    @Override
    public void init(BundleContext bc, DependencyManager dm) throws Exception {
        Properties props = new Properties();
        props.put(EventConstants.EVENT_TOPIC, "examples/events/greetings");

        dm.add(createComponent()
```

```
                .setInterface(EventHandler.class.getName(), props)
                .setImplementation(ReceiverExample.class));
        }

        @Override
        public void destroy(BundleContext bc, DependencyManager dm)
                throws Exception {
        }
    }
```

If an exception occurs in an event handler, the EventAdmin implementation is required
to handle the exception, and event delivery should continue. Most EventAdmin implementations log errors to the LogService if available. Some implementations, like the
one from Apache Felix, can blacklist misbehaving event handlers.

Aspect Services

Aspect Oriented Programming (AOP) can be very useful to dynamically add some new
functionality to existing code. This is often used to inject so-called cross cutting concerns
such as security, logging, and caching into code. Although a full AOP solution such as
AspectJ could be used in an OSGi environment, it is not necessary in most cases. In
most cases, we only need the concept of interceptors on services; e.g., intercept each call
to a service to add caching or perform additional security checks or logging. Although
there is not an out-of-the-box OSGi feature for this, we can use Apache Felix Dependency Manager to do this.

With Apache Felix Dependency Manager, an aspect is just another service with a higher
service priority than the original service. The original service is injected into the aspect
so that method calls can be delegated to the original service.

A trivial example is an aspect for LogService that rewrites each log message to upper-
case. The aspect just takes care of the uppercasing, while the logging itself is still delegated to the original service:

```
public class UppercaseLogAspect implements LogService{
    private volatile LogService logService;

    @Override
    public void log(int level, String message) {
        logService.log(level, message.toUpperCase());
    }

    @Override
    public void log(int level, String message, Throwable exception) {
        logService.log(level, message.toUpperCase(), exception);
    }

    @Override
    public void log(ServiceReference sr, int level, String message) {
```

```
        logService.log(sr, level, message.toUpperCase());
    }

    @Override
    public void log(ServiceReference sr, int level, String message,
            Throwable exception) {
        logService.log(sr, level, message.toUpperCase(), exception);
    }
}
```

Note that the activator is slightly different from an activator that registers a normal service:

```
public class Activator extends DependencyActivatorBase {
    @Override
    public void destroy(BundleContext bc, DependencyManager dm)
        throws Exception {
    }

    @Override
    public void init(BundleContext bc, DependencyManager dm)
        throws Exception {

        dm.add(createAspectService(LogService.class, null, 10)
            .setImplementation(UppercaseLogAspect.class));
    }
}
```

A consumer that uses LogService just injects LogService. The aspect is used automatically without the consumer knowing about this:

```
public class AspectTester {
    private volatile LogService logService;

    public void start() {
        logService.log(LogService.LOG_INFO, "some lower case log message");
    }
}

public class Activator extends DependencyActivatorBase {
    @Override
    public void destroy(BundleContext bc, DependencyManager dm)
            throws Exception {
    }

    @Override
    public void init(BundleContext bc, DependencyManager dm) throws Exception {
        dm.add(createComponent()
            .setImplementation(AspectTester.class)
            .add(createServiceDependency()
                .setService(LogService.class)));
    }
}
```

Although aspect services are only a very small part of AOP, they do offer a powerful mechanism to dynamically add behavior to existing services. Similar to servlet filters, aspects can be chained. The order of aspects can be controlled by setting a different service ranking on each aspect.

If you are familiar with EJB or CDI interceptors or Spring AOP, this should be very familiar as well.

The Bundle Cache

An OSGi framework has a persistent store where installed bundles and bundle state are stored. On Apache Felix, this folder is named *felix-cache* by default. Because of the bundle cache, all installed bundles in a framework will still remain installed after a framework restart. The bundle cache can be used to store data as well. You can access the bundle cache in code from the BundleContext. The following example serializes its state to the bundle cache when the bundle is stopped and deserializes it again when the bundle is started. Note that this survives framework restarts as well:

```
public class BundleCacheExample implements MessageLog {
    private static final String DATA_FILE_NAME = "greetinglog.ser";
    private volatile BundleContext context;
    private List<String> messageLog = new ArrayList<>();

    public void receiveMessage(String msg) {
        messageLog.add(msg);
    }

    @Override
    public List<String> listMessages() {
        return messageLog;
    }

    @SuppressWarnings("unchecked")
    /**
     * Serialize the list of messages to the bundle cache.
     */
    public void start() {
        File dataFile = context.getDataFile(DATA_FILE_NAME);
        if (dataFile.exists()) {
            try (FileInputStream fin = new FileInputStream(dataFile);
                 ObjectInputStream in = new ObjectInputStream(fin)) {
                messageLog = (List<String>) in.readObject();
            } catch (IOException | ClassNotFoundException exception) {
                throw new RuntimeException("Error deserializing greeting log",
                    exception);
            }
        }
    }
}
```

```
/**
 * Deserializes a list of messages from the bundle cache.
 */
public void stop() {
    File dataFile = context.getDataFile(DATA_FILE_NAME);
    try (FileOutputStream fout = new FileOutputStream(dataFile);
        ObjectOutputStream out = new ObjectOutputStream(fout)) {
            out.writeObject(messageLog);
    } catch (IOException e) {
        throw new RuntimeException("Error serializing greeting log", e);
    }
}
}
```

The example uses the Java Serialization API to write the list of messages to disk and to read the list of messages from disk when the bundle is restarted. Because this is bundle state, it makes sense to write the serialization file to the bundle cache. This is done using the BundleContext.getDataFile(String fileName) method; it returns a File instance that represents the file in the bundle cache. As a developer, you don't really have to know where the bundle cache is stored; the framework will take care of this.

CHAPTER 5

Pointers and Pitfalls

In the previous chapters, you have seen the most important OSGi features that you will need to build real applications. There are still a lot of OSGi topics that we haven't covered. The OSGi specification has been around for over 10 years, and some things have made in into the standards that turned out differently than expected and are better left untouched. This can be confusing to new users. Some features may even seem compelling at first. Therefore this chapter will discuss some of the features of OSGi that you should probably avoid.

Better Understanding OSGi Specifications

For someone new to OSGi, the phenomenon of OSGi specifications might be confusing. There are three different specification bodies relevant to users:

- OSGi Core Specification
- Compendium Services
- Enterprise OSGi

The OSGi Core Specification describes the OSGi framework itself and is implemented by implementations such as Apache Felix and Eclipse Equinox. For the most part, you will not need to know all the details of the specification to work with OSGi, but it does describe all the rules of lifecycles, wiring, services, and complex topics such as the resolver and subsystems in newer versions of the specification. At the time of writing this book, the *R5* specification is the latest version. The OSGi Core Specification moves rather slowly, and new features are only added if absolutely necessary. This is a good thing, because all other specifications are based on the Core Specification.

The Core Specification does not describe any integration with other technologies such as Java EE or specific OSGi services. For this, we have the Compendium Services and

Enterprise OSGi. Enterprise OSGi is a set of independent specifications that are focused on "enterprise" usage. Here we find integration with Java EE, some cloud technology, configuration management, and many other services that make building enterprise-oriented applications easier. The name Enterprise OSGi is confusing to developers familiar with Java EE. Java EE is generally implemented entirely by an application server, and developers can use any of those technologies on a compatible application server. Enterprise OSGi, on the contrary, is a set of more loosely coupled specifications. In general, a runtime will not support everything of the Enterprise OSGi specification. Some runtimes offer a subset of those specifications. Alternatively you can find stand-alone implementations of some specifications that can be used on top of other runtimes, which is a more modular approach. Some specifications are even overlapping. There are, for example, multiple dependency injection specifications. The fact that Enterprise OSGi is not an umbrella specification gives greater flexibility and makes it possible to develop new specifications much faster. In this book, we will use several Enterprise OSGi specifications such as JPA and JDBC integration, which we will discuss in a later chapter.

The OSGi specifications are developed by the OSGi Alliance. The specifications are publicly available, but to take part in the specification process, you have to be an OSGi Alliance member, which is unfortunately not free. However, drafts of new specifications are generally made public, and feedback on specifications by the community is highly appreciated. Reference implementations are often developed in open source as well.

Require Bundle

An OSGi feature that new users are often attracted to is the notion of bundle dependencies. In a previous chapter, we discussed that bundles should normally only import packages. With a package import, we do not know (or care) up front which bundle will take care of the export. This is true decoupling: we only depend on an interface, without any coupling to who or what exports and implements this interface.

A bundle dependency breaks this concept. A bundle dependency creates a dependency on the symbolic name and version of a bundle instead of exported packages. By doing so, there is a tight coupling between the two bundles; you can't replace the implementation of an API by replacing the bundle, because the dependency is only satisfied by the exact bundle defined in the dependency. This effectively throws modularity overboard.

The reason that new users are often attracted to this feature is that it is very similar to the dependency model of nonmodular Java. Under normal circumstances, Java developers often think about dependencies on libraries and frameworks instead of APIs of libraries and frameworks. When moving to OSGi, you should adapt to the much better control you have over dependencies, instead of falling back to nonmodular solutions such as bundle dependencies. Because, with the right tooling, you don't write package imports by hand anyway. There is also no development overhead in using fine-grained package imports instead of depending on whole bundles.

A bundle dependency can be created using the `Require-Bundle` manifest header. All packages exported by the required bundle are wired to the requiring bundle.

Fragment Bundles

Another OSGi feature that you should probably stay away from are *Fragment Bundles*. Fragment Bundles were introduced to facilitate shipping internationalized resources separate of application code. For example, a bundle could use property files for labels and other texts presented to a user. These property files could be available in multiple languages. Instead of adding all these language files to the bundle itself, you can deploy them in Fragment Bundles so that only the language that the user actually uses needs to be installed.

A Fragment Bundle attaches itself to a host bundle when the host bundle is resolved. The resources within the fragment are then treated as if they were part of the host bundle. Fragments use the classloader of the host bundle and do not have their own lifecycle; fragments don't support `Bundle-Activators`.

A fragment is created by using the `Fragment-Host` header, which specifies the host symbolic name and version. For example:

```
Fragment-Host: some.bundle;bundle-version=1.0
```

Separating application code from resources sounds like a really good idea, so why shouldn't you use fragments? The problem with fragments is their lifecycle. Or the lack of it to be more precise. While fragments are installed into the framework as separate bundles, they are attached more or less statically to the host bundle. Updating a fragment requires the host bundle to be refreshed before the updated resources are available.

Separating resources from application code can be done in a much more flexible way using OSGi services instead of relying on the module layer. An elegant way of solving this is to introduce a service that makes resources available to other services.

Loading Extra System Packages

System packages are the packages exported by the system bundle (the framework bundle). The system bundle normally exports most `javax.*` packages (`java.*` is implicitly imported). This is sufficient for most applications, but in some cases you will run into libraries that require `com.sun` packages, for example. This is obviously a bad practice, but there is not much you can do about this for external libraries.

The `com.sun*` packages (and others) are available in the JVM. However, by default they are not exported by the OSGi framework. With a little bit of extra configuration, we can force the system bundle to export the extra packages with the following BND instruction:

```
-runsystempackages: sun.reflect,org.w3c.dom.traversal
```

This BND instruction results in the following, standardized system property:

```
org.osgi.framework.system.packages = sun.reflect,org.w3c.dom.traversal
```

Profilers, Coverage Tools, and Bootpath Delegation

Profilers and coverage tools often need an *agent* to instrument your application to collect data. As an example, we will discuss the installation of the YourKit profiler (*http://bit.ly/15kjE9e*). In a non-OSGi environment, you would have to add the following VM parameter when starting your application:

```
-agentpath:<profiler directory>/bin/mac/libyjpagent.jnilib
```

Because of the classloader isolation in OSGi, this will not work. As soon as you execute any code in your application, after attaching the profiler, you will see errors such as:

```
NoClassDefFoundError: com/yourkit/runtime/Callback.
```

The reason for this is that OSGi will not allow the YourKit classes to be loaded magically. Instead, we have to tell the OSGi framework that these classes should be available. We can do this by delegating the classloading of these classes to the boot classloader. These classes will then be available to all classloaders, without the need for explicit import packages.

To do this, add the following to your run configuration in Bndtools:

```
-runproperties: org.osgi.framework.bootdelegation=com.yourkit.*
```

Let's look at another example; a code coverage tool. Code coverage tools measure the percentage of code covered by unit or integration tests. To do so, the code must be instrumented. Depending on the code coverage tool you use, this either happens during an extra compilation step or dynamically at runtime. In any case, this requires loading the code coverage tools' classes. The following example shows how to set this up for Atlassian Clover (*http://bit.ly/190UpNa*). Other coverage tools might require a slightly different setup, but in general, the same approach can be applied:

```
-runvm: -Xbootclasspath/a:${workspace}/cnf/lib/clover.jar
-runsystempackages: com_cenqua_clover
```

These properties add the *clover.jar* file to the boot classpath and make the package com_cenqua_clover available from the system packages.

Dealing with Non-OSGi Libraries

Because OSGi has become a common environment, a lot of open source projects already offer OSGi bundles that can be used directly in an OSGi environment. We have seen this is quite trivial to do, although it requires splitting APIs and implementation classes. Some libraries still do not offer OSGi support, however. What should you do in a situation where you want to use a library that isn't available as an OSGi bundle?

Many open source projects use Maven as their build tool. There is a Maven plug-in that integrates BND into the build process. BND will generate the required import and export headers as part of the build. The only thing required in the plug-in configuration is a list of packages that should be exported. Depending on the structure of the library, this is often trivial.

If the library was not built with Maven, or when you don't have access to the source code, Bndtools can help repackage the JAR. Bndtools creates a new project that contains the original JAR file and instructions to export some of the packages from the original JAR file.

In many cases, it's easy to fix the problem yourself by repackaging the code in an OSGi bundle. A good practice would be to always try to contribute the required changes back to the open source project in question. In most cases, the developers are happy to integrate this into their projects because it broadens their target audience and doesn't have any downsides for existing users. But it is not always that easy.

The problems start when libraries or frameworks need to do custom classloading or expect to be able to load resources such as configuration files from specific locations. These kinds of libraries and frameworks are often designed toward the "big classpath" environment, where each class in the system is visible by a single classloader. This is obviously not how OSGi works and can impose a difficult problem to deal with. If you are a framework developer, you can read the next few paragraphs that provide some tips on how to be a good OSGi citizen when it comes to class loading. If you merely want to use a framework that isn't modular, you're best off walking away from it and looking for alternatives. Remember that frameworks are just there to make development easier; they are not requirements to build successful applications. Of course we do not advise writing all your code without frameworks and reinventing the wheel for everything, but there are alternatives that work well in OSGi in most cases.

Transitive Dependencies

Some libraries and frameworks have a ridiculously long list of transitive dependencies. In a non-OSGi project, this can be considered a huge architectural risk. Maven, for example, will pull in transitive dependencies automatically, leaving you in classpath hell, with possibly multiple versions of the same dependencies if you're unlucky. In OSGi, this problem seems to be even more difficult to deal with. We have to add those dependencies to the container, and all the dependencies must be OSGi bundles. This can be a painful and long process to go through.

Luckily there is a better alternative in OSGi. If you need a library that is this messy, it can be better to package the library and dependencies within the bundle that needs them. This way we don't end up with all kind of dodgy exports, and we don't have to deal with the fact that dependencies might not be bundles. In OSGi, a bundle can contain other JAR files, and classes within those JAR files can be used by the bundle as if they were in the bundle itself. This way you isolate the problem of the messy library within a single bundle, making sure that you're overall architecture isn't hurt by this. Of course it's preferable to use libraries that take modularity into account correctly, but at least this is a way to work with less perfect dependencies without losing your own structure.

Classloading Problems in Libraries and Frameworks

Some libraries and frameworks are more cumbersome to work with in OSGi (or any modular environment). Libraries and frameworks that do custom classloading or rely on classpath scanning are difficult to work with in OSGi. Java EE is notorious for making this mistake.

The problem most often originates by the need of an extension mechanism and ways to find classes that should be picked up by the framework. OSGi has excellent ways to create extension points in your own frameworks, but Java and Java EE unfortunately don't. Because of this, most projects create some custom extension mechanism that requires runtime classpath scanning and runtime classloading. Runtime classloading is done when code uses constructions such as `Class.forName(somepackage.Some Class);` Because Java EE uses a hierarchy of classloaders, there is also often the need to use context classloaders. This is not well defined in Java, and most frameworks use some kind of multistep fallback mechanism to guess the right way to load classes.

Classloading in OSGi is very well defined; only classes that are in the bundle itself and classes explicitly imported can be loaded. This makes it impossible to scan the classpath for specific kind of classes (e.g., classes with specific annotations). Dynamic classloading also requires the right classloader (the bundle classloader) to be used.

When encountering these kind of frameworks, there are several things that can be done. Also remember that it might be easier to just look for alternatives instead. Hibernate, for example, is infamous for being hard to use in modular environments, while EclipseLink offers a JPA implementation that works well in OSGi.

In the remainder of this chapter, we will look into several steps that can be used to work around the problems described.

Passing the Bundle Classloader Manually

Many frameworks allow you to pass in a classloader manually instead of relying on the trickery that figures out the classloader automatically. If this is the case, you can call the API with the bundle classloader and work around the problem altogether. Of course, this is only possible if the framework APIs allow this.

Alternatively, you can try to set the context classloader manually. This is already in the area of black magic, but many frameworks try to use the context classloader as part of their fallback mechanism. Again, this only works if the framework uses this consequently, and there is not really a way to know without looking in the source code.

Handling Classpath Scanning

Classpath scanning should be considered a bad practice in any case. It is expensive and becomes more expensive with every class that you add. In OSGi, this is hardly possible because you can't just access classes in any bundle. Many frameworks that rely on classpath scanning also have an API for programmatic registration of "services" in the framework. If this is the case, we can write some code that tries to find interesting services in a more OSGi friendly way and register those using the framework's programmatic API.

Let's consider a simplified example based on the real-world scenario of using JAX-RS. The JAX-RS specification is part of Java EE and allows easy registration of RESTful web services. In Java EE, you can create a RESTful resource by adding some annotations to a Java class:

```
@Path("example")
public class ExampleResource {
    @GET
    @Produces("application/json")
    public MyClass demo() {
        return new MyClass(...);
    }
}
```

A Java EE container scans all deployed classes when the container is started. It will look at every single class file and check whether the @Path annotation is present. If the @Path annotation is present, the class will be registered as a JAX-RS resource. The container startup time obviously increases when more classes are part of the deployment.

In OSGi, this kind of classpath scanning is a very bad practice. The programming model of JAX-RS is really nice, however, so it would be very useful if we can use this within OSGi. Let's imagine that the JAX-RS implementation also has an API to add resources programmatically using the following API:

```
void addResource(Object resourceInstance);
```

Although this exact example is imaginary, you will find a similar method in most real-world JAX-RS implementations. If we could now introduce an alternative way to find our resource classes, we could write code to add these classes or instances to the framework using this `addResource` method.

The Low-Level Service API

In one of the previous chapters of this book, we told you not to use the low-level APIs to register and consume services. Instead, a dependency injection framework should be used in almost every case. To better understand why you shouldn't use the low-level API, you should have an idea how the API works. And of course there are some rare cases where you want to prevent having any other dependencies than the OSGi API itself, for example, while creating reusable, low-level libraries yourself.

Registering Services

Registering a service using the low-level API is not that difficult, as long as you don't depend on other services. Services can be registered using the `registerService` method on the BundleContext:

```
public class Activator implements BundleActivator {
    @Override
    public void start(BundleContext context) throws Exception {
        Dictionary<String, String> props = new Hashtable<>();
        props.put("myproperty", "myvalue");
        context.registerService(HelloService.class.getName(),
            new HelloServiceImpl(), props);
    }

    @Override
    public void stop(BundleContext context) throws Exception {

    }
}
```

A service can be registered in a similar way as we have done previously. There is no way, however, to declare dependencies on other services; these have to be retrieved from within the service code itself, which we will see in the next example.

Using Services

Using services is a lot more complicated than registering them. The reason for this is that we have to take care of service dynamics; services can come and go at any time. This complicates the code a lot if we have to check for deregistered services ourselves:

```
public class HelloConsumer implements BundleActivator {
    private volatile boolean running = true;
```

```
    @Override
    public void start(final BundleContext context) throws Exception {
        new Thread() {

            @Override
            public void run() {
                while (running) {
                    // 1 Get service reference
                    ServiceReference<HelloService> serviceReference =
                        context.getServiceReference(HelloService.class);

                    // 2 Check service reference
                    if (serviceReference != null) {
                        try {
                            // 3 Get service instance
                            HelloService service =
                                context.getService(serviceReference);

                            // 4 Check service instance
                            if (service != null) {
                                service.greet();
                            }
                        } finally {
                            // 5 Don't hold references to unused services
                            context.ungetService(serviceReference);
                        }
                    }

                    try {
                        TimeUnit.SECONDS.sleep(1);
                    } catch (InterruptedException e) {
                        e.printStackTrace();
                    }
                }
            }
        }.start();
    }

    @Override
    public void stop(BundleContext context) throws Exception {
        running = false;
    }
}
```

Let's walk through the numbered code comments:

1. Find a service reference for the given interface and filter. This is not a reference to an implementation yet. A reference is found when a service of this type and filter is registered.

2. Check whether a service was found.

3. Get an implementation reference for this service.

4. Check if the service wasn't deregistered before invoking it.

5. Make sure that the service instance can be garbage collected when the service is deregistered.

That's certainly a lot of complicated code. No wonder many developers think services are too complex! The code is now also full of OSGi specifics, instead of the clean POJO model that we have been using so far.

But once again, do not use these low-level APIs unless you absolutely have to.

Service Tracker

Service Tracker is a Core specification that offers a way to use services in a more convenient way, without depending on extra dependencies such as Apache Felix Dependency Manager. Using Service Tracker is still a lot less convenient than using a dependency injection framework. Only when a dependency on a dependency injection library would truly be a problem (e.g., when building a low-level framework) should you fall back to Service Tracker.

With Service Tracker, we can track the availability of services. The following is an example of a simple `BundleActivator` that tracks a Greeter service. When a Greeter is available, the example will keep on printing the `sayHello` message. When the Greeter service is not available, it prints `No greeter available`. When a Greeter is registered again, it will immediately be used again:

```
public class ServiceTrackerExample implements BundleActivator {
    private ServiceTracker tracker;

    @Override
    public void start(BundleContext context) throws Exception {
        tracker = new ServiceTracker(context,
            context.createFilter("(objectClass=" + Greeter.class.getName() +
                ")"), null);
        tracker.open();
        System.out.println("opened tracker");
        new Thread() {
            @Override
            public void run() {
                while(true) {
                    Greeter greeter = (Greeter)tracker.getService();
                    if(greeter != null) {
                        System.out.println(greeter.sayHello());
                    } else {
                        System.out.println("No greeter available");
                    }

                    try {
```

```
                    TimeUnit.SECONDS.sleep(1);
                } catch (InterruptedException e) {
                    e.printStackTrace();
                }
            }
        }
    }.start();

    }

    @Override
    public void stop(BundleContext context) throws Exception {
        tracker.close();
    }
}
```

Based on a service filter, we can create a `ServiceTracker`. The `ServiceTracker` takes care of handling service references; all we need to do is check for null of the actual service instance.

We can also use a callback model using Service Tracker, with methods that are invoked when a service is added, modified, or deleted. For this, we need to implement a `ServiceTrackerCustomizer`. The following example is similar to the previous example, but now uses callback methods to track the availability of the Greeter:

```
public class TrackerCustomizer implements ServiceTrackerCustomizer{
    private Greeter greeter;
    private BundleContext context;
    private final GreeterThread greeterThread = new GreeterThread();

    public TrackerCustomizer(BundleContext context) {
        this.context = context;
        greeterThread.start();
    }

    @Override
    public Object addingService(ServiceReference reference) {
        greeter = (Greeter) context.getService(reference);

        System.out.println("Greeter registered!");
        return greeter;
    }

    @Override
    public void modifiedService(ServiceReference reference, Object service) {

    }

    @Override
    public void removedService(ServiceReference reference, Object service) {
        System.out.println("Greeter deregistered!");
        greeter = null;
```

```
        }

        private class GreeterThread extends Thread {

            @Override
            public void run() {
                while(true) {
                    if(greeter != null) {
                        System.out.println(greeter.sayHello());
                    }

                    try {
                        TimeUnit.SECONDS.sleep(1);
                    } catch (InterruptedException e) {
                    }
                }
            }
        }
    }
```

The `ServiceTrackerCustomizer` is passed into the `ServiceTracker` constructor.

Dynamic Classloading

We have discussed package imports extensively. They provide a way to declare what other packages are required to be exported by other bundles for a bundle to become active. Package imports are static; they are defined (generated in most cases) at bundle build time. In most cases, this is great; it tells us exactly what dependencies a bundle has.

There are some corner cases where we simply don't know all the required packages up front. Enter the world of *dynamic classloading*.

A real-world example is the JDBC driver mechanism. You will learn to use JDBC in OSGi in Chapter 9, so for now, let's focus on the classloading mechanism. JDBC is designed to be used with different databases; the API is standardized, but to work with an actual database, you need a so-called *driver* specific to the database you are using. At some point in the code, the driver has to be loaded. Normally this is done using runtime classloading as shown in the following example:

```
    Class.forName("some.database.jdbc.Driver");
```

This is not a problem at first sight. Although BND will not recognize that the `some.database.jdbc.Driver` should be imported because it's just a `String`, we could simply add the `Import-Package` manually:

```
    Import-Package: some.database.jdbc
```

This works, but we lost the flexibility of JDBC. In most applications, the driver class name is not hardcoded as in the preceding example, but loaded from a configuration file or another external resource. In this case, we would have to rebuild our bundle that uses JDBC every time we swap driver implementations. This is not practical at all, of course. You could very well argue that the classloading mechanism in JDBC is a poor man's modularity solution (it is), but for some technologies, like JDBC, this is just the way it works, and thus we have to deal with that.

 Since JDBC 4.0, `Class.forName()` is no longer explicitly required in code, since the driver will use the Service Loader mechanism defined as part of Java SE 6. However, the underlying problem of dynamically loading classes remains the same, and for the JDBC samples used throughout this book, we stuck to the familiar `Class.forName()` mechanism as a means of illustrating that problem.

What we really need is to step away from static import packages for these kinds of corner cases. In OSGi, we actually have two different options for dealing with these kinds of situations: `DynamicImport-Package` and optional imports.

DynamicImport-Package

A `DynamicImport-Package` is an `Import-Package` that is resolved during classloading. In contrast to normal imports, a `DynamicImport-Package` does not have any effect on bundle resolution. This means that a bundle containing `DynamicImport-Package` headers will resolve, even if the required packages are not available. Only when code in the bundle tries to load classes from the dynamically imported packages will the framework check if these packages can be resolved. If the packages can be resolved, they are loaded, and a `ClassNotFoundException` is thrown otherwise.

The fact that a `ClassNotFoundException` can be thrown obviously brings us back to the usual runtime errors that we know all too well from non-OSGi applications. Dynamic classloading is something that should only be used in very specific cases, not as a convenient way around resolver issues!

Back to the JDBC example. Because package names in JDBC drivers don't follow a standard naming scheme, there is no way to know up front what packages we need to import dynamically; that was the whole problem to start with. The only thing we can do is dynamically load any package using a wildcard:

```
DynamicImport-Package: *
```

We can dynamically load any class now, but we should be aware of the possible classloading exceptions. To reduce runtime exception as much as possible, we should still try to declare as many imports using the `Import-Package` mechanism as possible. An `Import-Package` always has precedence over `DynamicImport-Package`. In other words, if we `Import-Package` a package, it will be part of the bundle resolution and doesn't have to be resolved dynamically.

Optional Import-Package

A very different, but related, mechanism is an optional import. A normal `Import-Package` can be made optional by adding `resolution=optional` to it. The following example imports `org.example` optionally:

```
Import-Package: org.example;version="[1.0,2)";resolution=optional
```

The effect of an optional import is that the bundle will still resolve, even if the imported package is not available. When the class is used while it is not available, a `ClassNot FoundException` will be thrown. This is dangerous! When an optional dependency was not resolved, it will not try to resolve the package again until the bundle is refreshed.

Why would anyone ever want to use this? Well actually, there are not really that many valid reasons. The idea is that a bundle might have some dependencies that are not always necessary. For example, some code paths might never be called when configured in a specific way. In that case, the code has a compile time dependency on a package that might never be used at runtime.

When code is crafted carefully to deal with the fact that some classes may or may not be available, this is OK. Optional imports should not be used to work around cases when the code *probably* doesn't use those classes. Using optional imports for code that is not crafted specifically for this purpose takes away the deterministic behavior of the resolver and puts us back in classpath hell.

PART II

Developing Cloud Applications

CHAPTER 6

Cloud Application Architecture

In the previous chapters, we discussed the basics of modularity and OSGi. In this chapter, we will discuss how these concepts and techniques are applied to building sophisticated cloud applications.

What exactly do we mean by *cloud applications*? This is the term that is nowadays used to describe modern (web) applications using concepts such as RESTful Web Services and NoSQL and that require an elastic form of scalability. Technically speaking, this doesn't have to do anything with the cloud per se, but these are concepts from the *cloud era* that we live in. Another term that is frequently used for these kinds of applications is *SaaS*, or Software as a Service offered over the Internet.

The architectural aspects we discuss should be seen as a blueprint extracted from real projects we have worked on in the past few years, and the advice set forward in this chapter could be looked at as battle-hardened best practices.

The approach we will discuss fits deployment in the cloud very well and has a lot of benefits in this area, but the architecture is just as usable for a traditional on-premise deployment.

Technology Stack

At a high level, we can look at a typical cloud application and define it as technologies stacked on top of one another, as depicted in Figure 6-1.

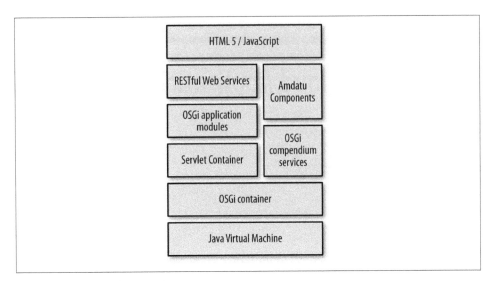

Figure 6-1. Technology stack

When aiming to build modern web applications, the approach is to expose RESTful Web Services that are consumed by client-side browser applications. The RESTful Web Services are implemented as OSGi services and use other application-specific OSGi services. All the code that you write will be packaged as OSGi bundles and will often be OSGi services, too. To focus on writing application code instead of infrastructure, we use standard OSGi services such as *HTTP Service, Log Service*, and *Configuration Admin*. Implementations for these services can often be found in the Apache Felix project, for example. For more high-level features such as integration with data stores, multi-tenancy support, and RESTful Web Services, we use facilities provided by the Amdatu project. The *Amdatu* project is an open source project where various OSGi components are available as building blocks focused on developing cloud applications.

The Amdatu Project

When building cloud applications, we need a lot more than just a modularity framework. We need tools to create things like RESTful Web Services, access NoSQL data stores, and handle security, just to name a few. The Java world has many different frameworks to help us with these things, but very little of them fit a truly modular architecture out of the box. Java EE and most other frameworks that feature desired implementations depend on OSGi bad practices such as classpath scanning.

Building everything from scratch is obviously also not something you should be doing. You should focus on writing actual application code instead of dealing with all kinds of low-level details. This is why the open source *Amdatu* project was started, back in 2010.

The Amdatu project (*http://www.amdatu.org*) contains all kinds of components (building blocks) focused on building cloud applications and makes these available under the Apache Software License 2.0. The goal of the project is to make modular application development as easy as possible. Amdatu has contributors from several companies that use Amdatu heavily in production. Many of the components found in Amdatu were originally developed as part of production systems and made open source after they proved to be useful.

Throughout the book, we will be using several Amdatu components for high-level APIs that we need.

The Layered Architecture

Over the past decades or so, it has become common to define an application in terms of layers. Every developer knows about the three-layer architecture as shown in Figure 6-2, and chances are high that you've seen systems with even five layers or more. Layers are about separating responsibilities of a system, where each layer focuses on a single technical task, while their functional areas might still be unrelated.

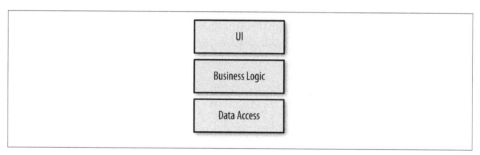

Figure 6-2. The typical three-layer architecture

Layers are great because it is never a good idea to mix different technical responsibilities in code. An important rule in a layered architecture is that layers are only allowed to call layers below them. The User Interface layer is allowed to call the Business Logic layer, but not the other way around. This is important to prevent tangles of *cyclic dependencies*.

Cyclic Dependencies

A cyclic dependency is when *A* uses *B*, and *B* uses *A*. Or in a more difficult scenario where multiple components are involved, such as shown in Figure 6-3.

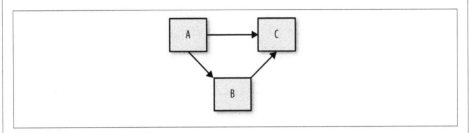

Figure 6-3. Example of a cyclic dependency

Cyclic dependencies are dangerous because it becomes very difficult to reason about the effect of code changes in such a situation.

When breaking down a system in modules, we still use layers as a mechanism to identify different technical parts of the system. However, in contrast to nonmodular solutions, we don't have to stop at those coarse-grained technical layers! Inside each layer we can identify separated parts by domain and/or functionality. This way, besides using horizontal slicing, we also introduce vertical slices to split up our code base. Let's use Figure 6-4 as an abstract example.

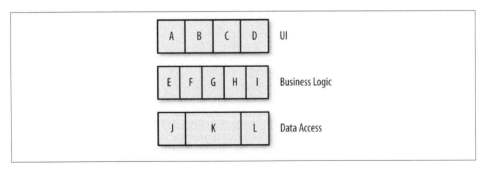

Figure 6-4. Layers of modules

Now, let's make this abstract model more concrete by looking at a simple example. We have a conference scheduling application that does the following:

- Lists information about sessions
- Tracks conference registrations
- Tracks session feedback

Each of these functional parts needs components in multiple layers; they each need a User Interface, a RESTful Web Service, some storage mechanism, and maybe some other services like sending email. Because we want to keep modules as small as possible, the functionally different parts should be isolated modules. The same can be said of the technical parts.

In Figure 6-5, each module is an OSGi bundle. This means that most bundles contain only a few classes and interfaces. A RESTful Web Service bundle might therefore even contain only a single JAX-RS annotated class. There is absolutely no problem with this; there is no runtime overhead, and creating a bundle is so easy that this shouldn't be a reason to not create many bundles. Every time you consider adding methods to an interface, you should ask yourself if these methods really belong in that service, or if they should be placed in a new service. When a service is doing something functionally unrelated, or technically unrelated, you should consider creating a separate bundle for this.

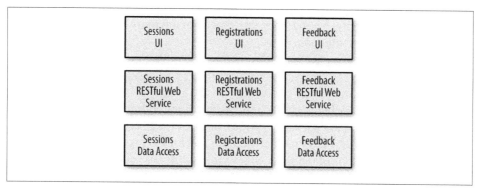

Figure 6-5. Modules of the conference scheduler example application

The benefit of small bundles is loose coupling and flexibility. Small bundles are easy to change because there's simply not that much code, so they are easy to understand. Ultimately it is even easy to just throw away a bundle and re-implement it if you are unhappy with it. This is a powerful tool. Throwing away code might sound like waste, but if it's about small amounts of code, it is often efficient to do so after gaining insights to a problem. This way you can always be focused on solving today's problems, without over-engineering for a future unknown. Create simple solutions to problems. When a solution becomes technical debt or isn't sufficient any more, just throw it away! *Modularity is the ultimate agile software development tool!*

Of course, this only works with well defined interfaces. Changing interfaces means a potential change to all other modules using this interface. Keep interfaces as stable as possible. If interfaces change, however, OSGi does give tools to indicate potential problems if we use semantic versioning on package exports. Bndtools has features to tell you what should happen to the export package version after making changes.

Inside a Bundle

Inside most of the bundles, there will be OSGi services. OSGi services are the core of our architecture, and we will create many of them. In a large application, it's not uncommon to have several hundreds of services. This is fine, because there is no runtime overhead in fully dynamic services.

Not all services have a Java interface. For example, a JAX-RS Resource (RESTful Web Service) should only be invoked using its HTTP interface. Because the class shouldn't be invoked by other Java classes, we don't have to define a Java interface. Other services, like data access services, should have a very well defined interface.

Always make sure that services are only doing work in a single technical layer. We often see examples where a service that started out as a data access service over time will contain more and more business logic that is unrelated to data access. If you notice this, you should refactor this code into a separate service. Services that become too large lose the benefits of modularity (because they aren't modular anymore) and will soon become hard to understand and maintain.

API Bundles

While it is perfectly possible to create bundles that have both exported API packages and private implementation packages, it is worth considering moving the API of a service to a separate bundle. The benefit of separate API bundles is that it is easier to have multiple implementations of the same API, or to replace a certain implementation entirely. On the other hand, you could argue that this doesn't happen very often. In any case, it is also always possible to move a package to another bundle. Because other bundles depend on the package (and not the bundle), you can apply this move without breaking anything.

Our own guideline is to always create separate API bundles, but you don't have to have a strong opinion on this. Both models work just as well, and it's mostly a matter of preference.

A good rule of thumb to decide if an API and implementation should be separated is to look at their expected maintenance cycle. If you expect that the implementation changes more often than its interface, it's mostly a good idea to separate them. In general, *rate of change* is a good criteria to apply to designing your system.

Separation of Concerns

Earlier in this chapter, we discussed that layers should never call services in technical layers higher than the layer the service resides in itself. For example, a data access component should never rely on code in the RESTful Web Service layer. Calling services in the same layer or layers at a lower level is perfectly fine, however. A service can also rely on several other services; there is no reason why a service could only rely on a single service. This way we can create composite services, services that create new functionality by combining data and functionality from several other (in general, lower-level) services. To be successful, it is crucial that services only do a single thing. This comes down to the *Single Responsibility Principle* or *Separation of Concerns*, as we learned in object-oriented programming.

When a service has more than one responsibility, it becomes harder to reuse the same service in a slightly different situation. Because of this, it is a best practice to split service code into small, low-level services, and combine those in a higher level service. This is obviously not something new; this has been a best practice since object-oriented programming became popular. Modularity makes this easier to reason about, however, which helps creating and keeping a clean design.

Depending on many existing services also has a downside. A module with many dependencies becomes less flexible in the sense that it becomes harder to reuse the module. Reusing becomes harder because all of its dependencies would be dragged in as well. On the other hand, only creating modules without any dependencies (or very few dependencies, for that matter) would force us to reinvent the wheel in every bundle instead of reusing existing code. This is obviously a difficult trade-off that we have to be aware of. Dealing with this brings us back to layering again. Create small reusable services with little dependencies to start with. These low-level services provide reusable building blocks in our application. At a higher level, we might define services that have dependencies on several lower-level services. This high-level service would be more difficult to reuse, but this is less of a problem since it has a very specific and narrowed-down task.

Services Are Responsible for Their Own Data

Another best practice is that services should be responsible for their own data. If we have a service that stores and retrieves data from a specific datastore, only this service should access that data. Other services should access the data through the service. If several services accessed the data directly, we would break modularity at the datastore level; we can't change the implementation of a module without potentially breaking other modules. A service's data must only be accessible through its service interface.

Bndtools Project Structure

Now that we have a bunch of modules defined, how would that translate to a Bndtools workspace? Bndtools has the possibility to create several bundles from a single project. This way you will have a slightly different development and deployment view, but that is absolutely fine. The end result is the same, no matter if bundles are created from a single project or multiple projects. Because of that, it's also easy to move code from a project that generates several bundles to a separate project if, for example, the bundle becomes larger.

As a general rule of thumb, it is convenient to put bundles that are in the same functional area in a single Bndtools project. These projects often have dependencies among them, and having them in a single project reduces build path configuration. It is also common to work on multiple layers of a single functional domain when adding functionality, so it's also a convenient grouping while developing.

Unrelated bundles should be created from different Bndtools projects to prevent the build path to become too cluttered.

For an example project, we could create a structure as shown below:

```
org.example.sessions
- sessions.api
- sessions.rest
- sessions.mongo
org.example.sessions.test
org.example.registration
- registration.api
- registration.rest
- registration.mongo
- registration.email
org.example.registration.test
org.example.feedback
- feedback.api
- feedback.rest
- feedback.stats
- feedback.mongo
org.example.feedback.test
```

You can imagine that some code in the `feedback` project depends on APIs from the `sessions` project. This is no problem; project separation is only a development view that should be convenient. It is by no means a runtime separation; all bundles will end up in the same OSGi container after all, with dependencies between them defined and managed by package imports and exports.

Comparing with SOA Again

By now it should be clear that an OSGi based modular architecture is something very different then SOA, although some of the design concepts are the same. The big difference is that OSGi services run in the same Java Virtual Machine; invoking a service is just a direct method call. In SOA, we would have to use messaging to invoke services. With OSGi services, we don't have the overhead (both during development and runtime) of messaging and all the difficulties this implies, while we still have loosely coupled components. Also note that it would be possible to create a SOA based system, where each component is built using OSGi services. They are simply on another level.

Remoting

We have seen that OSGi services live in the same Java Virtual Machine. There are a lot of benefits to this, but in some cases, we might want to distribute components to several virtual machines. Note that we do not require this for most web applications, even if they must be horizontally scalable, as discussed in the next chapter. In cases where we want to have two (or more) clearly separated systems, we need some kind of remoting mechanism to communicate between the two.

There are several options to do so:

- Using (RESTful) Web Services
- Using Messaging
- Using OSGi Remote Services

The first two options, RESTful Web Services and messaging, are technology agnostic. This is both the upside and downside of these solutions. The obvious advantage is that we could have components developed in different technologies (other than Java). The downside is that working with Web Services or messaging requires a very different approach compared to simply invoking methods on an interface. On the other hand, invoking a remote method is very different from invoking a local method, even if the code might look exactly the same. Remoting introduces a large performance penalty, which often requires a different interface granularity, and method arguments are *call-by-value* instead of *call-by-reference*.

OSGi Remote Services is an Enterprise OSGi specification that enables distributed OSGi services. This specification is focused on communication between remote OSGi services in a convenient way. The concept is not very different from older remoting solutions such as RMI and CORBA, but fits the OSGi services model better. The underlying transport protocol is implementation dependent. Some implementations even support remoting to native components. The Amdatu project is the reference implementation for OSGi Remote Services as specified in the Enterprise OSGi specification.

The main takeaway here is that both OSGi services and distributed components are ways to modularize a system. OSGi services are used at the micro-level of code modularization, while distributed modules are more at the macro-level. Both techniques can be used together, and one doesn't exclude the other.

CHAPTER 7

Architectural Capabilities

In this chapter, we will look at several important nonfunctional requirements and see how these are supported by the architecture that we discussed in the previous chapter. The main focus will be on a number of nontrivial system capabilities that are most affected by the nature of cloud computing, such as scalability. Obviously, there are many more nonfunctional capabilities than discussed in this chapter. We chose to leave out the nonfunctionals that are not any different when building traditional Java applications.

Maintainability

Maintainability is probably the system capability that benefits most from a modular architecture. Even very large code bases become understandable when divided in small isolated modules. We can change or completely replace implementations without having to worry that we break code that has a dependency on certain implementation classes rather than interfaces. As stated before, modularity is the ultimate agile tool.

Of course, we should be realistic and remember that there are many other aspects that influence maintainability. Even a highly modular system can be a maintenance nightmare if we have tangled, cyclic dependencies, no unit tests, and unreadable code, just to name few. Modularity is by no means an excuse to forget about other programming best practices. It does, however, give us maximum flexibility when it comes to replacing (pieces of) implementations.

Extensibility

Many systems require some kind of plug-in system. Even for SaaS applications, it is not uncommon to have customer-specific extensions. These extensions to the system should be loosely coupled from the core of the system and should be easy to integrate.

Plug-in systems are one of the traditional examples of OSGi. By combining techniques such as the *whiteboard* and *extender* patterns, we can easily create plug-in systems where plug-ins are deployed as separate bundles. That way we have loosely coupled extensions and flexibility at deployment time.

The reason this is different from plain Java or Java EE is that neither Java nor Java EE has a sufficient extension mechanism. Java has the notion of the `ServiceLoader` since Java 6, but this is a very limited (and hard to use) mechanism. The root of the problem is that the `ServiceLoader` is not modular by design, but is based on the concept of a single classloader that needs visibility to both the service interface and the implementation.

Scalability

When creating web applications, it is almost always important to design for scalability. Scalability covers two different topics:

- Being able to handle a certain amount of users
- Not using more compute resource than strictly necessary

The latter is also called *elasticity*: grow and shrink your environment for the current user load. Elasticity is one of the benefits of the cloud, and we will discuss this in more detail in Chapter 10.

A fair question to be asked is whether scalability really matters. Most applications never reach the massive scale like Twitter and Facebook. However, many applications will easily outgrow a single server, and that's when scalability becomes something to be aware of.

The holy grail in scalable applications is horizontal scalability. Horizontal scalability allows you to simply add more servers to scale up, without changing anything on the application or the way the application is deployed. Horizontal scalability is easy to accomplish with the best practices discussed so far and with what we will be discussing in this chapter. Of course, there are still some things to consider.

The biggest roadblock for horizontal scalability is session state. Session state is user-specific data stored in-memory on a web server for the duration of the HTTP session. An example of session data could be a user's shopping basket in a web store application. Sessions always had an important role in (Java) web applications, and they were almost always a *scalability killer*.

Because sessions are stored on the web server, it ties the user to that specific server. And that's a problem for horizontal scaling. Ideally, each individual web server should be able to handle any request from any user. Load balancers have some tricks for this, *sticky sessions*. The load balancer sends the user to the same server on every request based on a HTTP request header or cookie. This works but hurts failover capabilities. In case that specific web server goes down (maybe as a result of automatic scaling, or if some calamity happens), the session data is lost. Solutions have been invented for this as well, such as *cluster session replication*, which is a feature of many Java EE application servers. While they offer a solution, they also require a lot of infrastructural complexity and overhead, eventually leading to declining improvements in scalability when adding additional servers.

Although there are solutions to the problems introduced by sessions, by far the easiest way of solving them is by not using sessions at all. This may sound strange at first, given the fact that Java web applications relied on this in the past. It is very well feasible with the way we build web applications today, however. With the increasing power of web browsers, we can move parts of our application to the client side. As discussed before, our Java backend only publishes RESTful Web Services. Our web application can entirely be written in HTML 5 and JavaScript. Or maybe the application is a native iOS or Android application. This offloads all the logic related to rendering views and navigation to the client. With this, a lot of the reasons why sessions were traditionally used now disappear. Server side, we no longer care to know where the user is in the application; we just produce and consume data via RESTful Web Services. Many examples of session usage can now be offloaded to the client. For example, a shopping basket can be entirely client-side until the user decides to place an order.

Of course, this doesn't mean we are not allowed to store any data. We just don't deal with as much volatile data as we traditionally did. Any data that we do want to store can be stored directly in a datastore such as a NoSQL store. Another reason why sessions were traditionally used was to offload the database. Databases have always been hard-to-scale components in web architectures. Relational databases don't scale horizontally, which puts a hard limit on how many users can be handled by a database cluster. With NoSQL datastores, this issue is changed as well; some NoSQL datastores scale order of magnitudes better than relational databases. More on data access and the usage of NoSQL datastores can be found in Chapter 9.

However, a common question remains. How does our backend know which user requested data? A RESTful Web Service might return different data to different users. And typically, some RESTful resources might not be available to all users. Using sessions, this is traditionally solved by adding a cookie with a *session ID* to each request. The session ID is then used to load the correct session data, and the session might contain details about the user. We can apply a similar trick without using sessions. For this, we generate a token for a user and put that in a cookie. The backend can then use the token to retrieve user details either from the token itself (which is often an encrypted set of user data) or from a datastore (or cache) backing the application. A ready-to-use implementation of this token mechanism can be found in *Amdatu Security* and is discussed in Chapter 8.

Given these technology changes, we don't really need to rely on the session anymore. When an application doesn't use the session at all, that application is considered stateless. In a stateless architecture, we can simply add more servers to our infrastructure, and each server will add linearly to the amount of users we can handle. This makes scaling and deployment almost as easy as deploying to a single server. This fully eliminates complex cluster setup and administration!

So how does modularity help scalability? In most cases, it doesn't matter; a monolithic application might just be as scalable as a modular application. We do have some very useful tools to enable automatic scaling in the OSGi world however, and they will be discussed in Chapter 10.

Testability

With rapidly changing code bases and eager dependency management, testing becomes a prime aspect of the application architecture. The ability to be *testable* is an often overlooked aspect in a number of traditional frameworks. Both modularity in general, and OSGi as a framework, help a lot to improve testability. When we speak of testing, we should distinguish between several levels:

- Unit tests
- Integration tests
- Functional tests

For unit testing, it is important that code doesn't contain too many references to framework (implementation) classes, and especially no static method calls to a framework. References to implementation classes make it impossible to mock these dependencies, which makes unit testing very difficult. When working with OSGi, you will only have dependencies on OSGi interfaces, never on framework implementations. Basically you would have to do something very much the wrong way to end up with dependencies on framework implementation classes. Because we only use interfaces, mocking becomes extremely easy. The other benefit of a modular architecture is that we are forced to use interfaces for all our services as well. We simply can't do the wrong thing, and this greatly improves testability of our code.

Integration testing means different things to different people. When we talk about integration testing, we talk about testing a (small) set of components running within a real OSGi framework, and potentially using a real database. Integration testing does not mean testing the fully integrated application as a whole, because tests like these are very difficult to maintain. Integration testing becomes a lot easier with a modular architecture. The major difficulty for nonmodular applications is bootstrapping only part of the application. In an integration test, it is undesirable to bootstrap the complete application, because we should focus on testing only a small set of modules in each integration test.

Although in the traditional world, the Arquillian (*http://arquillian.org*) test framework is an excellent solution for testing parts of code in-container, it still requires a quite complicated setup. This is because we have to define modules (or *micro-deployments*, as Arquillian calls them) as part of the test scenarios. Solving classloading issues is often part of setting this up. This is obviously not a problem of Arquillian, but a problem of nonmodular code bases in general.

With a modular architecture, we already have clear module boundaries. The only thing left to configure is a run configuration that lists the set of bundles that should be installed as part of the test. More details about integration testing can be found in Chapter 4.

Functional tests (either automated or manual) require a fully bootstrapped application in general. A modular architecture doesn't really make this any harder or easier.

CHAPTER 8

Creating Web Applications

Now that we have a firm understanding of what it takes to create a modular design and how we can bring such a design toward the runtime, it is time to start working on some real examples. As the title of this book suggests, we are guiding you toward taking modular concepts to the cloud, as this is the most important area of focus for modern web application development. The aim of this chapter is to take you on a tour across the various options that are out there for creating modern web applications in a modular way.

Modular Web Applications

A valid question to ask is what use it is exactly to start modularizing web applications. Just like with any application, the notion of having an improved logical and physical structure in the form of modules makes for easier maintenance and deployment. Then, the lifecycle management and service dynamics enable you to control what is available and when. Lastly, the concept of services support loose coupling, making it easy to swap implementations without changing a single line of client code. All things considered, a modular web application enjoys the following benefits:

- Encapsulated modules
- Versioning semantics
- Class space isolation
- Declarative dependencies
- Dynamic refreshing and updating (hot class reloading)

HTTP Service

The Core OSGi specification doesn't have any facilities for building web applications, but within the list of OSGi Compendium Services, the HTTP Service provides a way of registering servlets, filters, and resources under named aliases. Incoming URI requests are matched against those aliases and will be redirected to the published services.

Dealing with the HTTP Service in your application is pretty straightforward. You can look up the HTTP Service from the service registry and interact with the HTTP Service programmatically. The HttpService interface provides methods to register and unregister servlets or static resources like images and HTML pages. The following code example uses the HTTP Service to register a number of static resources on a given alias:

```java
public class ResourceRegistration {
    private volatile HttpService httpService;
    private volatile LogService logService;

    public void start() {
        try {
            httpService.registerResources("/", "/html", null);
            httpService.registerResources("/images", "/images", null);
        } catch (NamespaceException ne) {
            if (logService != null) {
                logService.log(LogService.LOG_WARNING,
                    "Failed to register resources.", ne);
            }
            else {
                ne.printStackTrace();
            }
        }
    }

    public void stop() {
        httpService.unregister("/");
        httpService.unregister("/images");
    }
}
```

The ResourceRegistration class depends on two services that we need to resolve in a corresponding Activator class. The HttpService should be marked as required because without it, the ResourceRegistration class cannot do much useful work. The LogService can be declared optional though:

```java
public class Activator extends DependencyActivatorBase {

    @Override
    public void init(BundleContext context, DependencyManager manager)
            throws Exception {

        manager.add(createComponent()
```

```
                    .setImplementation(ResourceRegistration.class)
                    .add(createServiceDependency()
                        .setService(HttpService.class)
                        .setRequired(true))
                    .add(createServiceDependency()
                        .setService(LogService.class)
                        .setRequired(false)));
        }

        @Override
        public void destroy(BundleContext context, DependencyManager manager)
                throws Exception {
        }
    }
```

In order to test our `ResourceRegistration` service, we need some actual content in the JAR file as well. For this, we create both an *html* and an *images* folder in the project. The *html* folder contains a very simple *index.html* page, and the *images* folder holds the Jetty logo. The content of the *index.html* page is as follows:

```
<html>
<head>
    <title>Home</title>
</head>
<body>
    <h1>Hello World!</h1>
    <p>powered by:
    </p>
    <img src="/images/jetty_logo.png">
</body>
</html>
```

The next thing that we should do is make sure that our static content ends up in the JAR file. To make this work, we add an extra manifest header called `Include-Resource` to the bnd file. In Bndtools, you can do this on the Source tab of the *bnd.bnd* file:

```
Include-Resource: html=web-resources/html,\
    images=web-resources/images
```

The first value in the value pair represents the location within the generated JAR file where the resources will end up. The value after the equals sign refers to the location of the files in your project.

Now Bndtools makes sure that every time the JAR contents gets generated, our static content will be included as well. To check that the contents end up in the right place within the JAR file, you can use the JAR File Viewer in the Bndtools perspective in Eclipse. Double-clicking the JAR file under the *generated* folder in your project also works.

Final thing to worry about is firing up the OSGi framework with all the required bundles included. In order to have the HTTP Service present, we need to find an implementation of the HttpService. Apache Felix provides one using an embedded Jetty web server. Include the following bundles in your run configuration:

- osgi.cmpn
- org.apache.felix.dependencymanager
- org.apache.felix.http.jetty
- org.apache.felix.log (optional—only if you want the LogService to be present)

 If you run into any trouble along the way, optionally include the Gogo shell and the Apache Felix Dependency Manager shell along with the other bundles in order to figure out what is wrong.

The Apache Felix HTTP Service implementation will make Jetty available on port 8080 of the local machine by default. Taking into account how we mapped the resources using the ResourceRegistration service, we can now access our page at: *http://localhost: 8080/index.html*.

Taking It One Step Further with Servlets

Servlets seem to be a nice first step when thinking beyond serving static resources. Using the HTTP Service, it is also possible to register servlets by calling the register Servlet method on the HTTP Service instance.

There is nothing special about servlets being served from OSGi bundles. The following code example is just a basic *javax.http.Servlet*:

```
public class HelloWorldServlet extends HttpServlet {

    @Override
    public void doGet(HttpServletRequest request, HttpServletResponse response)
        throws ServletException, IOException {
        PrintWriter out = response.getWriter();
        out.println("Hello from Servlet!");
    }
}
```

The ResourceRegistration service should then be amended so that it includes a call to the registerServlet method of the HTTP Service:

```
httpService.registerServlet("/hello", new HelloWorldServlet(), null, null);
```

The `registerServlet` method accepts four parameters:

- Servlet alias
- Servlet instance
- An additional configuration `Map`
- An optional `HttpContext`

The servlet alias must begin with a slash (/) and must not end with a slash. The servlet instance can be provided by creating a new instance of the servlet class you want to register. Optionally, an additional configuration map containing parameters for the servlet can be specified. If present, the contents of the map will be copied to the `ServletContext` object. Finally, you can specify a specific `HttpContext` object in case you want to override how to handle authentication, mime types, and resource mapping.

Now, after saving changes in the IDE, the servlet has become available on the specified URI. Point the browser to *http://localhost:8080/hello* and admire your work.

Instead of registering the servlet by hand, which is considered to be a bad practice, the whiteboard pattern (See Chapter 3) can be put to use again. In this case, the whiteboard implementation simplifies the task of registering servlets by exporting them as services. The whiteboard implementation will detect all `javax.servlet.Servlet` and `javax.servlet.Filter` services when the right service properties are specified.

Instead of manually registering the servlet in our `ResourceRegistration` class, we switch our attention to the activator class and add the following code snippet to register our servlet as a service:

```
Properties servletProps = new Properties();
servletProps.put("alias", "/helloworld");

manager.add(createComponent()
    .setInterface(Servlet.class.getName(), servletProps)
    .setImplementation(HelloWorldServlet.class));
```

The whiteboard implementation for the Apache Felix HTTP Service is in a different bundle. In order for it to pick up servlet registrations, make sure to add the bundle `org.apache.felix.http.whiteboard` to the list of run requirements. As soon as the bundle is added to the runtime, it starts picking up servlet registrations. This will make the servlet available on *http://localhost:8080/helloworld*.

Adding Filters into the Mix

Filters were introduced in the Java Servlet specification 2.3 and introduce a component type to dynamically intercept requests and responses to transform or use information contained within them. Filters typically provide cross-cutting concerns that can be "attached" to any type of servlet or JSP page.

Typical use cases for filters include:

- Logging and auditing
- Security related features such as triggering authentication
- Encryption mechanism to protect sensitive data traveling between client and server
- Compression mechanism for speeding up downloads
- Transformation of data contained in the original request or response

The following code example represents a simple intercepting filter that lists the remote host address before the request will be passed on to the target servlet:

```
public class LoggingFilter implements Filter {

    @Override
    public void init(FilterConfig filterConfig) throws ServletException {
    }

    @Override
    public void doFilter(ServletRequest request, ServletResponse response,
        FilterChain filterChain) throws IOException, ServletException {
        String ip = request.getRemoteAddr();
        System.out.println("Incoming request from " + ip + " at " +
            new Date().toString());

        filterChain.doFilter(request, response);

        System.out.println("Sending response to " + ip + " at " +
            new Date().toString());
    }

    @Override
    public void destroy() {
    }
}
```

Just like with servlets, we can register the filter whiteboard-style using the activator class. A filter needs one required property that defines the pattern to which the web server will match the filter. The following code snippet shows how this can be done:

```
Properties filterProps = new Properties();
filterProps.put("pattern", "/helloworld");

manager.add(createComponent()
    .setInterface(Filter.class.getName(), filterProps)
    .setImplementation(LoggingFilter.class));
```

Handling Web Resources Automatically

The Amdatu Web components extend the standard OSGi HTTP Service using the whiteboard pattern. Amdatu Web is a collection of pluggable bundles that provide convenience support for static resources and also JAX-RS RESTful resources (as we will see in the remainder of this chapter). Later in the book, we will be using a number of other convenience features from Amdatu Web.

The Amdatu Resource Handler is one of the bundles in the Amdatu Web project, and it allows you to easily serve static resources from a bundle. All you need to do is to add two extra manifest headers to the bundle:

```
X-Web-Resource-Version: 1.0
X-Web-Resource: path/to/resources
```

The Amdatu Resource Handler bundle implements the extender pattern (see Chapter 4) and will pick up these manifest headers and register them at the supplied alias. This saves us the trouble of manually registering them as resources with the HTTP Service as we did in the previous examples in this chapter. You have to make sure though that the static content that you want to be served is packaged as part of the bundle. As discussed in the beginning of this chapter, this can be done using the `Include-Resource` manifest header, like this:

```
Include-Resource: html=web-resources/html,\
    images=web-resources/images
```

Rethinking Web Applications

Although it is pretty straightforward to get some servlets, filters, and static resources up and running in a modular fashion, developing web applications in the form of plain old servlets by hand feels like setting the clock back for at least 10 years. In traditional web development, we would now search for comfort in the hands of some well-known (third-party) web frameworks. Mind you, since we are running in a modular environment, they are generally not an option, since their centralized controllers break the concept of modularity, and many of them rely upon reflection and dynamic class loading. Some web frameworks such as Wicket or Vaadin have a more modular setup from themselves and are therefore more suitable candidates. Another alternative would be to still use a nonmodular web framework but limit its scope to a single module. Of course, with the latter approach, you can question modularity of the application in general. Although for some use cases this might be an option to consider.

However, with the cloud in mind, we might have to reconsider what a typical web application looks like today. With the rise of cloud applications comes the eventual decline of server-side web frameworks. Depending on what kind of application you are building, you might require a heavy user interface. Nowadays web applications leverage the processing power of the client's web browser for two reasons: first, because it contains a very powerful rendering engine capable of almost anything, and second, because running the user interface on the client offloads the burden on the server. For this reason, we see a fundamental shift of web frameworks on the server being replaced by considering the server an API to talk to from the client. If you consider the server part of the application an API accessible over the Web, then you need to have a way of consuming the server's services in a way that behaves like the Web. This is exactly the idea behind REST and HTML 5 style client-side JavaScript frameworks.

RESTful Web Services

REST, or Representational State Transfer, is an architectural style for building web applications introduced by Roy Fielding in 2000 that describes a set of principles for using the Web's standards, such as HTTP and URIs, in a natural way. Since the mid-2000s, the usage of REST has exploded, and therefore it can nowadays be seen as a standard way of defining APIs over the Internet. REST fits cloud applications very well, because it allows you to interact with clients as diverse as mobile phones, browsers, and other websites with minimal overhead. In theory, REST is not tied to the Web, but it is almost always implemented as such, and as a result, REST can be used wherever HTTP can.

By no means is this chapter a full introduction to REST. If you would like to read more about its background and details, we kindly refer to *RESTful Web Services* (O'Reilly), written by Leonard Richardson and Sam Ruby or *RESTful Web Services Cookbook* (O'Reilly), written by Subbu Allamaraju.

REST is another example of where we don't want to reinvent the wheel and come up with our own implementation based on plain servlets, or on top of some shady, third-party framework. REST on the Java platform has been properly standardized in JAX-RS, the Java API for RESTful Web Services, and this is exactly what we want to use. Using the Amdatu project, we can. Amdatu offers REST support for OSGi by wrapping the Apache Wink (*http://wink.apache.org*) implementation of the JAX-RS standard in a ready-to-use component.

Getting Started

Let's start with building a very simple *Hello World* style RESTful service to explain the concepts of adding REST to modular applications. For this, we return to Eclipse and Bndtools and we create a new bundle descriptor. You can choose whether to add it to the existing project or create a separate new Bndtools project for it. Let's call the bundle descriptor *rest*. In order to get started with REST in an OSGi environment, we need to include the Amdatu JAX-RS component *org.amdatu.web.rest.jaxrs* to the build path of our project. Now we can use the familiar JAX-RS annotations in our code, and once deployed, they will be picked up by the runtime.

Create a new Java class called `HelloWorldResource` and put it in a package called `web.rest`. This class will represent our RESTful Resource, and to register it as such with the runtime, we annotate the class with the JAX-RS `@Path("hellorest")` annotation. Next, add a new method to the class that returns a simple string ("hello world" or something similar, of course). The method should be annotated with `@GET` and `@Produces(MediaType.TEXT_PLAIN)`. This is all that needs to be done to complete our first RESTful service. Your code will look similar to this:

```
@Path("hellorest")
public class HelloWorldResource {

    @GET
    @Produces(MediaType.TEXT_PLAIN)
    public String sayHello() {
        return "Hello RESTful, modular, world!";
    }
}
```

The resource will be registered whiteboard-style with the runtime. In order to deploy our resource in the system, we use the familiar activation mechanism. Therefore our resource will be treated as an OSGi service. Create a new `Activator` class in the same package as the `HelloWorldResource`, and use the Apache Felix DependencyManager to initialize the following service:

```
manager.add(createComponent()
    .setInterface(Object.class.getName(), null)
    .setImplementation(HelloWorldResource.class));
```

As you can see from the code snippet, the interface of the RESTful resource is set to `Object`. No other service within our system will look up the implementation directly. In order to interact with this service, we use HTTP instead.

To complete our first RESTful service, we go to the Contents tab of the *rest.bnd* Bundle Configuration file and drag the *web.rest* package into the Private Packages part. Also make sure that the `Activator` class we just created is listed as the activator for this bundle. Next up is completing the Run Configuration. In order to get the required RESTful services runtime, we need an HTTP server (Jetty, that you might have already added from a previous example), the whiteboard implementation, and finally, we need JAX-RS and Apache Wink, which we take from Amdatu REST. Resolve all the Run Requirements and Save the configuration file. The following list of bundles should now be added to your run configuration:

- `org.apache.felix.http.jetty`
- `org.apache.felix.http.whiteboard`
- `org.amdatu.web.rest.jaxrs`
- `org.amdatu.web.rest.wink`

If everything is fine, you will notice some output appearing in the console indicating that Jetty is running. Check the list of bundles in the console with the `lb` command to see if our *web.rest* bundle is deployed. Now, open a web browser, navigate to *http://localhost:8080/hellorest*, and admire your first modular RESTful service.

Port and context conflicts
The Apache Felix HTTP Service implementation will make Jetty available on port 8080 of the local machine by default. Make sure you don't have any other service running on that port already. Alternatively, the port setting can be changed by using Configuration Admin. Please refer to the online documentation of the Apache Felix HTTP Service for the exact naming of the service properties.

Implementing an Agenda Resource

In Chapter 3 you created a simple conference agenda implementation. Here we continue that example by creating a RESTful resource on top of that. All we know is the interface of the agenda. We don't care about its implementation, as the runtime will take care of that. The RESTful resource that we will be creating in this paragraph takes whatever is returned from an agenda implementation and converts it to JSON. JSON, or JavaScript Object Notation (*http://www.json.org*) is the easy, light-weight protocol of choice for REST services these days. As an added bonus, this transport format can also be easily manipulated from JavaScript on the client side. This way, we have a means of exposing our services and their data as a RESTful API over the Internet, making it convenient for all sorts of clients to interact with the backend of our application.

Create a new Bndtools project and add a class called `AgendaResource` in a package called `agenda.rest`. Annotate this class with `@Path("agenda")` and add a method, annotated with `@GET`, to list the conferences from the agenda. In this method, you will be using an object mapper to map Java objects to JSON, and vice versa. There are multiple ways of doing this, but the Jackson ObjectMapper (*http://bit.ly/17k6vli*) is a popular choice. To be able to use the Jackson mapper, we need to add two more bundles to our build path:

- `jackson-core-asl`
- `jackson-mapper-asl`

Also make sure you have all the bundles from the previous exercise, as they are still required to do REST.

To make this resource do something useful, we need a reference to an actual agenda service. Add a `volatile` field to the `AgendaResource` to hold the reference to this service. Now use this service reference to retrieve the list of conferences and map them to JSON using the `ObjectMapper`. Since the output of our method will be JSON, we have to set the right `MediaType` using the `@Produces` annotation. As our method produces a list of type `Conference` from within the agenda resource, we must alter the URI path by adding another annotation `@Path("conferences")` on top of our methods. After following all the instructions, your code will end up looking something like this:

```
@GET
@Path("conferences")
@Produces(MediaType.APPLICATION_JSON)
public String listConferences() throws Exception {
    ObjectMapper mapper = new ObjectMapper();
    return mapper.writeValueAsString(agendaService.listConferences());
}
```

Next thing is to add the creation of this service in an `Activator`. This code will look a lot like the one we used to register the `HelloWorldResource` in the previous example. However, in order to have the new resource return the list of conferences, we need a service dependency to the agenda service. This should also be marked as a required dependency, because when there is no agenda implementation available, this resource cannot function properly. The resulting `Activator` code will look like this:

```
manager.add(createComponent()
    .setInterface(Object.class.getName(), null)
    .setImplementation(AgendaResource.class)
    .add(createServiceDependency()
        .setService(Agenda.class)
        .setRequired(true)));
```

Drag the *agenda.rest* package in the Private Packages on the Contents tab and Save all your work. The end result of our work can be seen in the browser. Navigate to *http://localhost:8080/agenda/conferences*and check whether the conferences are returned in JSON format.

JSON formatting

In our example, the `conference` type is just a simple structure having two simple properties, but as you can tell from the output, readability of JSON types can quickly become an issue. For most browsers, there are plug-ins or extensions available that offer nice formatting for JSON structures.

Extending the Agenda Resource

To make the Agenda Resource even more useful, we are going to add a method to it to add a new conference to the list of conferences held within the backing Agenda service. Therefore we need to add a method that takes a String variable as input, and we use the Jackson mapper the other way around to convert this incoming JSON into Conference Java objects. The code for such a method will look like this:

```
@POST
@Path("conferences")
@Consumes(MediaType.APPLICATION_JSON)
public void addConference(String conference) throws Exception {
    ObjectMapper mapper = new ObjectMapper();
    agendaService.addConference(mapper.readValue(conference, Conference.class));
}
```

The code example has some particular differences with the listConferences method that we wrote earlier. First, it is using @POST instead of @GET, as we will now utilize HTTP's POST command to send data to the server. The second difference is that @Consumes now indicates the supported MediaType for this method. Finally, there are the obvious differences in the method signature and the JSON mapping.

There is no need to redeploy things, as all changes in the code are automatically reloaded upon save. Now to test posting to our newly added method, we need the help of the curl command-line tool. If you are working on Mac OS X or Linux, this will be already installed on your system. If you are using Windows, you can download cURl for Windows (*http://bit.ly/16RhJwx*) or use another REST client tool or browser-based plug-in. Using curl, we can issue the following command:

```
curl -i -H "Content-type: application/json" -X POST
-d "{\"name\":\"JavaOne\",\"location\":\"San Francisco\"}"
http://localhost:8080/agenda/conferences
```

This sends an HTTP POST message to the server that has the content type set to JSON and has a payload consisting of a JSON structure representing the Conference type. On the server-side, our resource should pick this up, and using Jackson, the body gets converted into a Conference type. Subsequently this conference will then be added to the list of conferences contained in the agenda service implementation. You can test if it works by pointing the browser to *http://localhost:8080/agenda/conferences*again, which should now return our freshly added conference as well.

Simplified Object Mapping

Another nice benefit of the Amdatu Web components is that they provide automatic marshaling of JSON to Java objects, and vice versa. Under the covers, it uses the Jackson mapper like we did in the previous examples, but instead of doing this manually, it registers a provider within Wink that will take care of this for us. In order to have the automatic marshaling, we need to add the `org.amdatu.web.rest.jackson` bundle to our run configuration. This bundle will automatically register itself with Wink. As a result of this, all of the object mapping can be stripped, and we no longer have to deal with clumsy strings but can use real types instead. The resulting code is very clean and concise and no longer holds the boilerplate mappings:

```
@Path("agenda")
public class AgendaResource {
    private volatile Agenda agendaService;

    @GET
    @Path("conferences")
    @Produces(MediaType.APPLICATION_JSON)
    public List<Conference> listConferences() throws Exception {
        return agendaService.listConferences();
    }

    @POST
    @Path("conferences")
    @Consumes(MediaType.APPLICATION_JSON)
    public void addConference(Conference conference) throws Exception {
        agendaService.addConference(conference);
    }
}
```

Self-Documenting RESTful Endpoints

Amdatu ships with a bundled version of the Swagger documentation framework (*http://bit.ly/15gZO5D*). This basically allows REST endpoints to document themselves. All you have to do is deploy the following set of bundles with your application:

- `org.amdatu.web.rest.doc`
- `org.amdatu.web.rest.doc.swagger`
- `org.amdatu.web.rest.doc.swagger.ui`

Once deployed, point your browser at *http://localhost:8080/ui/index.html* to see all the endpoints that have registered themselves with the REST runtime. You can drill down into any of them, inspect all their methods and parameters, and even invoke them directly from your browser.

Without doing anything yourself, there is just some basic documentation available. However, to add extra information about your services, you can use the provided annotation `@Description("This is a description.")` where it makes sense: methods, parameters, etc. They will be picked up and shown in Swagger automatically:

```
@Path("agenda")
public class AgendaResource {
    private volatile Agenda agendaService;

    @GET
    @Path("conferences")
    @Description("Returns all conferences as a list of type Conference.")
    @Produces(MediaType.APPLICATION_JSON)
    public List<Conference> listConferences() throws Exception {
        return agendaService.listConferences();
    }

    // ...
}
```

Modularizing RESTful Resources

Deciding how to structure your code into modules is of course very application specific, and it's impossible to come up with a blueprint that works best for every application. As a rule of thumb, you can use the following guidelines as a starting point:

- Each JAX-RS endpoint is deployed in a separate bundle.
- Don't write any reusable code in JAX-RS endpoints.

Let's say we have an endpoint /speakers and an endpoint /conferences. Both endpoints can be deployed in separate bundles for maximum reuse. The code related to storing and retrieving the data from a datastore should be deployed in separate bundles and exposed as OSGi services. This way we could reuse the Java API without deploying the RESTful web services. Take Figure 8-1 as an example.

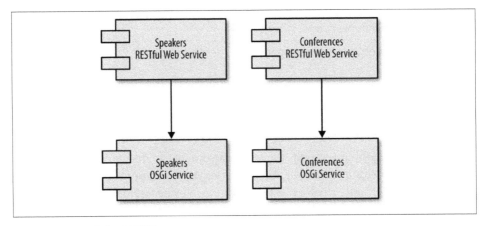

Figure 8-1. Modular REST resources

Modular User Interfaces Using HTML 5

Now that you have seen how to construct the backend services of our cloud application, it is time to discuss how modularity applies to the user interface part of our application. Currently, a number of HTML and JavaScript framework combinations are in vogue. The authors of this book have a particular interest in AngularJS, which is very popular at the time of writing this book.

Modern JavaScript applications become larger and larger, and we can easily end up with thousands of lines of JavaScript code. Bundling all this code together would impose the same problems as with Java. Most applications, however, have clearly separate functional areas. For example, a web shop has a customer facing part and a part only accessible to the owners of a shop. The shop owner's part could again be separated into order processing, product management, mailing lists, etc. Instead of looking at the web shop client application as one big application, we could modularize the application on features. The user interfaces for product management and order processing could be two different modules, for example. We can simply create those two user interfaces as two different AngularJS applications and package them in different bundles. An end user doesn't have to notice this at all; all the user sees is different pages in a browser.

The different parts of the application would be registered to different URL paths. For example, the order-processing user interface could be registered to */orders*, while the product management user interface could be registered to */productmanagement*. This doesn't require anything special, but some questions remain:

- How to deal with shared resources (like CSS and images)
- How to create navigation between modules
- How to deal with shared client state

To create user interfaces with an uniform look and feel, it's often desirable to use the same stylesheets and images for different parts of the application. How do we deal with this if we package the application in separate bundles? A common approach would be to package the shared resources in a separate bundle that makes the resources available on a URL that can be used by all other parts of the client application. For example, we could have a shared resources bundle that registers resources at */webresources*, such as */webresources/css/theme.css*. Another bundle could simply link to this URL, without even knowing it comes from another bundle:

```
<link rel="stylesheet" type="text/css" href="/webresources/css/theme.css">
```

Creating menu structures with links to different parts of an application works in a similar way. The menu could be part of the shared web resources bundle. The links to different parts of the application could just be hardcoded if parts of the application are not added/removed dynamically during normal operation. Although this is not truly dynamic, it covers most production situations well enough. In a more complex scenario, we could introduce a service that discovers active user interface parts so that we could add and remove parts dynamically. Each bundle containing a part of the user interface could register a service with the URL to that part of the application. Another bundle could listen for these services and make the current list available in a RESTful resource. The user interface could watch this resource and add/remove menu items accordingly. Whether these kinds of dynamics are required depends entirely on the use case.

Token Based Security

When building web applications, some sort of authentication and authorization mechanism is almost always required. It's also something very application specific; do users log in using an application-specific username and password using form-based authentication, or can they use providers such as Google and Facebook? The area of authentication is really too broad to discuss in this book, but there is one component that we do want to show: Amdatu Security.

The idea behind Amdatu Security is to put an abstraction between the actual authentication and authorization mechanisms and the application code. In our application code, we often need to check if a request comes from an authenticated user, and we need to get details from that user for further authorization. The Amdatu Security component provides a token provider. The token provider can generate tokens for a set of user details. The token is generated and encrypted using a private key and can't be forged (easily) by an attacker.

The token is generally generated when a user is authenticated successfully, using whatever authentication mechanism you use. The generated token is then stored in a cookie and sent to the server for each subsequent request. The server can use the token provider to decrypt the token and retrieve the user details from the token. With these user details, you can use your custom authorization mechanism to check if the user has the correct access permissions to continue.

Generated tokens must be stored somewhere. The implementation available in Amdatu Security is based on MongoDB, but you can plug in custom implementations as well.

Using the Token Provider

To use the token provider, you need to install the following bundles:

- `org.amdatu.security.tokenprovider.api`
- `org.amdatu.security.tokenprovider.impl`
- `org.amdatu.security.tokenstorage.mongo`

Make sure that the Amdatu MongoDB component is installed and a database is configured (as discussed in Chapter 9).

The TokenProvider must be configured with a secret key that is used to encrypt and decrypt tokens. The PID of the ManagedService is org.amdatu.security.tokenpro vider. The secretkey property should either be a 16-character key, or the exact string, [randomkey].

The following example uses the Google Plus API to authenticate using a Google account. This is just an example, and you can use any other kind of authentication mechanism as an alternative.

First, some JavaScript that is required for the Google Plus API. There is nothing Amdatu-specific in here. When a user is logged in successfully, a POST to the /rest/googlelogin service is executed, containing the user's details:

```
gapi.client.load('plus','v1', function() {
    var request = gapi.client.plus.people.get({'userId': 'me'});

    request.execute(function(resp) {
        resp.access_token = authResult['access_token'];
        jQuery.ajax({
            url: '/rest/googlelogin',
            type: "POST",
            data: JSON.stringify(resp),
            contentType: "application/json",
            success: function(response) {
                window.location.href='/index.html';
            }
        });
    });
});
```

The important part of the example is the RESTful web service that takes care of generating a token:

```
@Path("googlelogin")
public class LoginResource {
    private volatile TokenProvider tokenProvider;

    @POST
    @Consumes("application/json")
    public Response googleLogin(GoogleUser user)
        throws TokenProviderException {
        SortedMap<String, String> userMap = new TreeMap<>();
        userMap.put(TokenProvider.USERNAME, user.getId());
        userMap.put("googletoken", user.getAccess_token());
        String token = tokenProvider.generateToken(userMap);

        return Response.ok().cookie(
            new NewCookie("amdatu_token", token)).build();
```

```
    }

    @GET
    @Produces("text/plain")
    public String getGoogleAuthToken(@Context HttpServletRequest request)
        throws TokenProviderException, InvalidTokenException {
        String token = tokenProvider.getTokenFromRequest(request);
        SortedMap<String, String> tokenProperties =
            tokenProvider.verifyToken(token);

        return tokenProperties.get("googletoken");
    }
}
```

That's all we need. The `amdatu_token` cookie is now set, and the GET method shows how to validate an existing token and retrieve properties from it. With these properties, we can implement our own authorization mechanism without relying directly on the Google APIs.

Web Application Bundles

An alternative way of dealing with the Web in a more modular way is present in the form of so-called Web Application Bundles. A Web Application Bundle, or WAB for short, is an OSGi bundle that contains a web application and that can be deployed in an OSGi container. Essentially it is a good old WAR (Web Archive) file behaving as an OSGi bundle.

The Web Application Bundle is a relatively new standard in the Enterprise OSGi specification. WABs are defined in the OSGi Version 4.2 Enterprise Specification.

You use a WAB in an OSGi application in much the same way that you use a WAR file in a typical Java enterprise application. For example, you use a WAB to host servlets, static content, or JSPs as part of your application.

A WAB contains OSGi metadata, for example, a manifest header, `META-INF/MANI FEST.MF`, so that you can use the familiar features that OSGi provides. For example, you do not need to package dependencies inside a WAB, since you can declare import constructs in the OSGi metadata.

The simplest form of a WAB consists of a bundle containing three files:

• Java servlet class representing the web application
• Web deployment descriptor (*web.xml*)
• OSGi manifest file

Since the WAB is a special-purpose WAR file, it is defined by the structure within the archive. No required filename extension is specified by the specification, so it can be named anything, but *.war* or *.wab* or *.jar* are most common.

Besides the usual OSGi headers, the OSGi manifest must contain a special header, Web-ContextPath, specifying the web application's context path:

```
Web-ContextPath: hello
```

 Alternative Header

Some containers implementing the WAB standard do also require a second header called Webapp-Context. For some strange reason, adding this second header to the manifest and setting it to the same value as the Web-ContextPath is the only way to make it work.

A number of Java EE compatible application servers offer support for Web Application Bundles. At the time of writing, all major Java EE application servers support WABs except for Oracle WebLogic®.

One of the nice things about the Web Application Bundle is that it is treated as a *true* Java EE web application. Therefore it has access to the JNDI context of the application, allowing it to integrate with other Java EE components in the server. Another advantage of using an OSGi-enabled server runtime is that you can take advantage of the runtime services offered, such as clustering for load balancing and failover. Of course, this advantage only has any value if your deployment environment is an application server.

OpenSocial

OpenSocial is a specification written by the OpenSocial Foundation, with members coming from IBM, Jive, Google, and other companies. The OpenSocial specification was supposed to bring standardization to the field of social networks. There are two main features in the specification:

- Standards and APIs to define profiles, relations, etc.
- A gadget platform

iGoogle was one of the best known implementations, and there are several other products using OpenSocial (even Jira), but unfortunately the standard never really took off. Google announced discontinuation of iGoogle in favor of Google+, which is not based on OpenSocial. So why discuss a not-so-successful social networking standard in a book about modularity? This is because the gadget platform that is part of OpenSocial offers some very nice modularity aspects to frontend development that might still be of use today.

A gadget is a self-contained application that can run in an OpenSocial dashboard. With iGoogle, you have a personal dashboard where you can add gadgets that show the weather, the news, your email, etc. A gadget has two states in most cases: one for when the gadget is shown together with other gadgets on a dashboard, and one for when the gadget is opened full screen. Gadgets are pure HTML/JavaScript applications, which is perfect for modern web applications. Most examples of gadgets are quite simple (e.g., showing the weather). However, it is possible to create very sophisticated JavaScript applications using this technology, and this is how we use OpenSocial ourselves.

If the dashboard paradigm fits your application, OpenSocial is a nice way to create this in a modular way. At the same time, OpenSocial is much more than just a dashboard, and basing your application on OpenSocial just to get the modularity benefits is probably excessive.

Getting Started

The Amdatu project has an OpenSocial container implementation based on Apache Shindig that works well in an OSGi environment. Before this becomes useful, one would have to develop a dashboard. This is nontrivial, and out of the scope of this book. The Amdatu OpenSocial component also has an example dashboard that shows how you could create a dashboard yourself.

To bootstrap the Amdatu OpenSocial container, we need the following bundles to be installed:

- `org.amdatu.opensocial`
- `org.amdatu.opensocial.dashboard.demo`
- `org.apache.felix.dependencymanager`
- `org.apache.felix.configadmin`
- `org.apache.felix.http.whiteboard`
- `org.apache.felix.http.jetty`

When the framework is started with these bundles, you should be able to access the dashboard on *http://localhost:8080/index.html*. There are some demonstration gadgets availalbe that you can try to see if the dashboard is working.

Creating Gadgets

An OpenSocial container becomes a lot more interesting when you can register your own gadgets. Amdatu OpenSocial uses the whiteboard pattern for dynamic gadget registration.

The whiteboard mechanism listens for (de)registrations of the `org.amdatu.open social.gadget.Gadget` interface.

To create a gadget, we will need two things:

- A *gadget.xml* file that contains the gadget metadata and its HTML
- An activator that registers the gadget

A *gadget.xml* (you can actually name it whatever you want) is an XML file with some metadata about the gadget, and the gadget contents itself. OpenSocial defines multiple views of a gadget because gadgets can behave differently when shown on the dashboard together with other gadgets. The following example defines a view for both maxi mized and minimized states:

```
<Module>
    <ModulePrefs title="Book Gadget" description="Example gadget from the book"
        author="Paul Bakker and Bert Ertman" width="640" heigth="2000">
    </ModulePrefs>
    <Content type="html" view="canvas">
    <![CDATA[
The book gadget's maximized view.

    ]]>
    </Content>

    <Content type="html" view="home">
    <![CDATA[
The book gadget's minimized view
    ]]>
    </Content>
</Module>
```

The content itself is just HTML. You can add or include JavaScript and CSS like in any normal web page.

Next, we need to register the gadget with the container:

```
import org.amdatu.opensocial.gadget.Gadget;
import org.amdatu.opensocial.gadget.SimpleGadget;
import org.apache.felix.dm.DependencyActivatorBase;
import org.apache.felix.dm.DependencyManager;
import org.osgi.framework.BundleContext;

public class Activator extends DependencyActivatorBase {

    @Override
    public synchronized void init(BundleContext context,
        DependencyManager manager) throws Exception {
        Gadget gadget = new SimpleGadget("BookGadget", "/book/gadget.xml");
        manager.add(createComponent()
            .setInterface(Gadget.class.getName(), null)
```

```
            .setImplementation(gadget));
    }

    @Override
    public synchronized void destroy(BundleContext context,
        DependencyManager manager) throws Exception {
    }
}
```

The example uses the convenience `SimpleGadget` class that takes a gadget *ID* and a *URL* where the *gadget.xml* is available. To make the *gadget.xml* file available, we can use the Amdatu Resource Handler as discussed previously in this chapter:

```
Include-Resource: book=static
X-Web-Resource-Version: 1.0
X-Web-Resource: /book
```

Your gadget should now be available on the dashboard.

Java Portlet Specification

The Java Portlet Specification (JSR 168 and JSR 286) is a Java specification focused on portals/dashboards. The high-level concept is the same as for OpenSocial dashboards: create many small applications that can be used together in a single environment. This solves modularity at the same level as well; by creating many small portlets instead of one big web application, you already introduce a high level modularity principle. However, in contrast to OpenSocial gadgets, the portlet specification defines how gadgets should be built at the server side. This doesn't fit modern web applications well, and Portal servers are hard to use and often heavy weight products. Although portals do offer some modularity, we advise against using them.

CHAPTER 9

Persistence

This chapter will cover interacting with persistent storage services. It will discuss a variety of ways to interact with the different types of storage available to cloud applications, such as relational databases and NoSQL stores. Next, it will show you how to use these kinds of storage from a modular application.

Relational Databases

The relational database has been part of enterprise applications for the last two decades. For most applications, it is the default choice for storing persistent data. Relational databases offer familiar concepts for storing data using the concepts of tables and rows.

In order to use a relational storage mechanism, a schema has to be defined up front. The schema defines the layout of the tables and how they interconnect to other tables using referential integrity mechanisms such as foreign keys.

The table design is such that data will be normalized, meaning that we structure the tables in such a way that avoids duplication or redundancy. Yet, there is a trade-off between normalization and development ease-of-use. If normalization is taken too far, it will be quite hard to work with the data model, especially with Object/Relational Mapping frameworks.

The main way of interacting with the database is through the use of a structured query language called SQL. SQL is pretty much standardized in a way that there is a general subset of commands and constructs that is shared across almost all databases. Sometimes a particular database offers a SQL dialect in a way that adds extra functionality on top of the standard part.

Using SQL, you can read, insert, update, and delete data in the database. It also has the concepts of transactions in which you can combine multiple SQL operations into an atomic set of operations that will execute isolated from other activity. Transactions in a relational database offer so-called *ACID* properties. ACID is an acronym that stands for atomic, consistent, isolated, and durable. ACID provides us with a safe environment in which to operate on data:

Atomic
> Each transaction is all or nothing. All operations in a transaction succeed, or every operation is rolled back.

Consistent
> On transaction completion, the database is structurally sound. Each transaction will bring the database from one valid state to another.

Isolated
> Transactions do not contend with one another; contentious access to state is moderated by the database so that transactions appear to run sequentially. As a result, the outcome of incomplete transactions (transactions that are still in progress) is not visible to other transactions.

Durable
> The results of applying a transaction are permanent, even in the event of failures. To defend against failures, the outcome of a transaction must be stored in non-volatile memory (i.e., disk).

The result of these principles is that once a transaction completes, its data is consistent and stable on disk.

Interacting with a relational database from Java can be done using JDBC or an Object/Relational Mapping framework. We will explore both ways in the next few paragraphs. Before we will dive into the details though, one essential difference between the regular usage of relational databases and the usage of relational databases in a modular fashion has to be made. In a modular application, each module should be responsible for maintaining its own data. This is fundamentally different from what is common with relational databases in regular applications, where most of the times the application as a whole has a single schema. Because a single schema would lead to very tight dependencies between modules, it should be avoided.

JDBC

Java Database Connectivity, or JDBC for short, is a standard API that comes with the Java Development Kit for interacting with a relational database. It offers a set of classes and interfaces that mimic constructs in the database, such as SQL statements (SELECT, INSERT, UPDATE, and DELETE), and result sets.

Update statements such as INSERT, UPDATE, and DELETE return an update count that indicates how many rows were affected in the database. These statements do not return any other information. Query statements return a JDBC result set. Individual columns in a row are retrieved either by name or by column number. There may be any number of rows in the result set. The row result set has metadata that describes the names of the columns and their types.

Using the JDBC API from a modular application is pretty much straightforward, but there is a gotcha in loading the database drivers. In JDBC, depending on the specific database vendor (MySQL, PostgreSQL, Oracle, etc.), a specific driver is needed to implement the vendor-specific interface to the database. This vendor-specific implementation is hidden behind the standard `Driver` interface. This Service Provider Interface (SPI) programming practice that is often used in Java APIs and of which JDBC driver loading is a prime example, presents a little challenge. The JDBC Driver interface is a common interface, but the name of the class implementing it is unknown and might differ in specific driver cases. Because our bundle can only see classes in packages it imports, how can it import anything from an unknown package? To work around this issue, OSGi has the `DynamicImport-Package` manifest header, which represents a comma-separated list of packages needed at runtime. Because the package name may be entirely unknown, it is also possible to use a wildcard (*) to match everything. A generic dynamic import will look like this:

```
DynamicImport-Package: *
```

Using such a very generic import directive will import any package needed by the bundle. Alternatively, they may be more limited to the specific packages that you wish to import such as:

```
DynamicImport-Package: com.mysql.*
```

Dynamic Classloading

More on dynamic classloading can be found in "Dynamic Classloading" on page 86.

Very precise declarations make less sense, since the general use case for dynamic import packages is for unknown classes. Dynamic import packages should therefore only be used as a last resort, since exposing everything on the classpath to the bundle essentially breaks modularity. In general, using `DynamicImport-Package` must be seen as a bad practice, except for situations where dealing with SPI, such as loading the JDBC Driver implementation.

After dealing with loading the correct database driver, all that is left is to supply the database driver implementation at runtime. Some vendors already offer their drivers as an OSGi bundle, e.g., MySQL. If the JDBC driver for your database is not available as an OSGi bundle, obtain the default driver JAR and wrap it in an OSGi bundle (see "Dealing with Non-OSGi Libraries" on page 79). The bundle must export the packages that are required for interacting with the database server. The bundle must also import the packages that it references:

```java
public class JdbcApplication {
    private static final String dbUrl = "jdbc:mysql://localhost:3306/test";
    private static final String dbUser = "user";
    private static final String dbPassword = "password";

    public void start() {
        Statement stmt = null;
        Connection con = null;
        try {
            Class.forName("com.mysql.jdbc.Driver");
            con = DriverManager.getConnection(dbUrl, dbUser, dbPassword);
            stmt = con.createStatement();

            ResultSet rs = stmt.executeQuery("SELECT * FROM contacts");
            while (rs.next()) {
                int id = rs.getInt("id");
                String name = rs.getString("name");
                String phone = rs.getString("phone");
                System.out.println("\tid=" + id + "\tname=" + name +
                    "\tphone=" + phone);
            }

            con.close();
        } catch (ClassNotFoundException e) {
            e.printStackTrace();
        } catch (SQLException e) {
            e.printStackTrace();
        }
    }
}
```

The code example shows how to load the correct driver for the MySQL database first, which resolves at runtime because of the dynamic import. Then it attempts to obtain a connection to the database using the MySQL driver and the supplied connection parameters. Finally, the JDBC API is used to emit a SQL query on the database directly and manually map the results back to Java data structures in memory, and simply print the results. Alternatively, JDBC can also be used to execute stored procedures in a database.

DataSource implementations, the recommended way to talk to databases in enterprise applications, are generally unaware of the various drivers used by the application. However, the driver class for a specific database must still be visible to the implementation to be able to make connections to the database, otherwise, a ClassNotFoundExcep tion will occur. With plain OSGi, nothing is offered to support DataSources. Within the OSGi Enterprise Specification, a different solution is provided: the JDBC Service interface. This interface contains methods for creating Driver, DataSource,

`ConnectionPoolDataSource`, and `XADataSource` objects. In short, anything you may want from an enterprise point of view is available, and this should be the way to go. However, there aren't many implementations of this enterprise specification yet; and therefore to enjoy it, you might have to implement it yourself.

Object Relational Mapping with JPA

Another form of interacting with relational databases from Java is through the use of Object/Relational Mapping (ORM) frameworks. An ORM framework maps the concepts of the relational model back and forth on a Java object model in memory. It uses a metamodel that contains the mapping information. An ORM framework is a very complex beast. Not all such frameworks fit modularity very well.

In Java, the standard for such ORM frameworks is JPA, which is short for Java Persistence API. JPA offers a standardized API for interacting with data in the database, and a pluggable model for so-called *persistence providers*. Popular persistence providers include *Hibernate* and *EclipseLink*.

Gemini JPA is a distribution of the EclipseLink JPA provider infrastructure that allows for it to be used in a modular environment. It currently supports OSGi and is an implementation of the OSGi JPA Service specification, part of the OSGi Enterprise Specification. If you want to use JPA in an OSGi environment, then Gemini JPA is something you can work with. In the next section of this chapter, we will show examples of how to use it. We will show some basic examples based on information taken from the Gemini JPA online documentation at the time of writing. Make sure to check the most recent version of the Gemini JPA online documentation when you decide to use it for your own application.

To use Gemini JPA, you will need to install the Gemini JPA bundle as well as the bundles it depends on. Besides the `org.elipse.gemini.jpa` Gemini JPA bundle and `javax.persistence` (JPA), the following EclipseLink bundles are also required:

- `org.eclipse.persistence.asm`
- `org.eclipse.persistence.antlr`
- `org.eclipse.persistence.core`
- `org.eclipse.persistence.jpa`
- `org.eclipse.persistence.jpa.jpql`

 You do **NOT** need the `org.eclipse.persistence.jpa.osgi` bundle shipped with EclipseLink. It contains an early version of EclipseLink support for OSGi which predates the OSGi JPA specification work. It is no longer supported, and developers should not use it.

Once these bundles have all been installed, the dependencies that you specify in your application must be properly specified. The first thing you must declare is a dependency on the set of JPA 2.0 `javax.persistence` packages that you use. When importing the JPA packages, the OSGi standard recommends that the `jpa` attribute be set to **2.0** to indicate the correct version of the JPA specification. The EclipseLink `javax.persis tence` JAR does the exporting using this attribute. An example application import is:

```
Import-Package: javax.persistence;jpa="2.0";version="1.1.0", ...
```

If EclipseLink specific APIs are used, then additional EclipseLink package dependencies may also be required.

When using JPA, you start by defining a so-called *persistence unit*. When defining a persistence unit, there are a few differences when using Gemini JPA in OSGi, as opposed to traditional JPA in a classpath-based environment. Traditional JPA dictates that a persistence descriptor called *persistence.xml* must be placed in the *META-INF* folder of a JAR file. In OSGi, the limitations are not as stringent, and the file may be given any name and placed anywhere in the *persistence bundle*, with the persistence bundle being referred to as the bundle containing the persistence unit. The caveat is that a special manifest header, the `Meta-Persistence` header, must be added to the *META-INF/MANIFEST.MF* file. The value of the header should be the name of the descriptor file, with its location relative to the root of the bundle. Multiple descriptors can be specified defining multiple persistence units. If the traditional *META-INF/persistence.xml* descriptor name and location are used, then the `Meta-Persistence` header entry can be left with an empty value entry. The default descriptor, if it exists, is always added to the set of descriptors that are specified in the `Meta-Persistence` headers. The following are examples of valid `Meta-Persistence` entries:

Meta-Persistence: `META-INF/persistence.xml`
>   Uses the default descriptor and (redundantly) indicates the name and location.

`Meta-Persistence`
>   Assumes the default *META-INF/persistence.xml* descriptor. Note that one or more spaces may need to be used as the value to satisfy the manifest parser.

Meta-Persistence: `META-INF/jpa.xml`
>   Specifies a file named *jpa.xml* located in the *META-INF* folder of the bundle. If *META-INF/persistence.xml* also exists in the bundle, then the persistence units defined in it will also be processed.

Meta-Persistence: `jpa1.xml, jpa2.xml`
>   Specifies two persistence descriptors, *jpa1.xml* and *jpa2.xml*, both located in the root of the bundle. If *META-INF/persistence.xml* also exists in the bundle, then the persistence units defined in it will also be processed.

The contents of the persistence descriptor for the most part follow the typical contents of a traditional *persistence.xml* file in a Java SE environment. The following rules apply:

- The transaction type should be RESOURCE_LOCAL (if specified).
- If the mapping-file element is used, the entry must be relative to the root of the bundle.
- Entities should be enumerated in class elements.
- The javax.persistence.jdbc.{driver,url,user,password} properties must be used to specify the JDBC connection properties.
- In addition, EclipseLink-specific properties can be used as described in the EclipseLink documentation.

Gemini JPA needs a JDBC driver to access the underlying database. Just like with plain JDBC, the driver class can be imported using a DynamicImport-Package header in the manifest.

In our example, we configure the persistence unit using a file called *jpa.xml* in the root of our persistent bundle. It contains the following settings:

```
<?xml version="1.0" encoding="UTF-8" ?>
<persistence xmlns:xsi="http://www.w3.org/2001/XMLSchema-instance"
    xsi:schemaLocation="http://java.sun.com/xml/ns/persistence
    http://java.sun.com/xml/ns/persistence/persistence_2_0.xsd"
    version="2.0" xmlns="http://java.sun.com/xml/ns/persistence">
    <persistence-unit name="myPU" transaction-type="RESOURCE_LOCAL">
        <provider>org.eclipse.persistence.jpa.PersistenceProvider</provider>
        <class>entity.Contact</class>
        <properties>
            <property name="javax.persistence.jdbc.driver"
                value="com.mysql.jdbc.Driver" />
            <property name="javax.persistence.jdbc.url"
                value="jdbc:mysql://localhost:3306/test" />
            <property name="javax.persistence.jdbc.user" value="user" />
            <property name="javax.persistence.jdbc.password" value="password" />

            <!-- EclipseLink specific properties -->
                <property name="eclipselink.ddl-generation" value="create-
tables" />
            <property name="eclipselink.ddl-generation.output-mode"
                value="database" />
        </properties>
    </persistence-unit>
</persistence>
```

Here are a couple of important things:

persistence-unit name

myPU is the name of the persistence unit that we should use as a filter in order to obtain the correct `EntityManagerFactory`.

transaction-type

Can only be `RESOURCE_LOCAL` since JTA transactions are not supported.

provider

Gemini JPA only supports EclipseLink as the underlying JPA Persistence Provider.

class

Lists the `Contact` entity as part of this persistence unit. In our case, it is just one element, but there can be many `class` elements listed here. Wildcards can be used as well.

Finally, a number of JPA and EclipseLink specific properties are specified to configure the JDBC driver and schema generation strategies.

Our database still contains a table called `contacts` that holds a number of names, email addresses, and phone numbers. With ORM, we mimic the relational model in an Object Oriented model. JPA calls them *entities*. In our simple example, we model a `Contact` object after the `contacts` database table:

```
@Entity
@Table(name="contacts")
public class Contact {

    @Id @GeneratedValue
    private Long id;

    private String name;
    private String email;
    private String phone;

    public Contact() {
    }

    public Contact(String name, String phone) {
        super();
        this.name = name;
        this.phone = phone;
    }

    // Getters and setters omitted for brevity...

    @Override
    public String toString() {
        return "Contact [id=" + id + ", name=" + name +
            ", email=" + email + ", phone=" + phone + "]";
```

```
        }
    }
```

The `@Entity` and `@Id` annotations are mandatory and required by the JPA specification. They indicate to treat this class as an entity and identify the field that should be used as the primary key. With `@GeneratedValue`, we indicate that the value of the primary key would be determined by the database at the time of record creation. In the case of MySQL, a *sequence table* will be used to determine the next available value. With `@Table`, we provide some additional mapping information, such that EclipseLink can map this class to the correct table in the database.

When a persistence bundle gets installed, the persistence units it defines will be discovered and processed by Gemini JPA. Gemini JPA will register the `EntityManager Factory` service in the OSGi service registry for each persistence unit found in the bundle.

The `EntityManagerFactory` (EMF) service is the service that is typically looked up and used by JPA users. It will be registered under the fully qualified name `javax.persis tence.EntityManagerFactory` with the properties described in Table 9-1.

Table 9-1. EntityManagerFactory properties

Property name	Property value
osgi.unit.name	Name of the persistence unit
osgi.unit.version	Bundle version of the persistence bundle
osgi.unit.provider	Class name of assigned provider
osgi.managed.bundles	Bundle ID of the persistence bundle

The EMF service will only be registered if the JDBC driver is accessible. Gemini JPA will check for JDBC accessibility in two ways. First, it will use the `javax.persis tence.jdbc.driver` property to look for a `DataSourceFactory` service in the service registry. If the service is not found, then a local load will be attempted, meaning that Gemini JPA will attempt to load the driver directly from the persistence bundle. If unsuccessful, no EMF service will be registered for the persistence unit.

Gemini JPA users will normally look up the EMF service by specifying the name of the `EntityManagerFactory` class and filter it with the persistence unit `name` property. The following example method illustrates how this can be done in the activator:

```
@Override
public void init(BundleContext context, DependencyManager manager)
    throws Exception {
    manager.add(createComponent()
        .setInterface(Object.class.getName(), null)
        .setImplementation(JpaApplication.class)
        .add(createServiceDependency()
```

```
            .setService(EntityManagerFactory.class, "(osgi.unit.name=myPU)")));
    }
```

Be aware that under some circumstances, the EMF service might become unregistered. Users may want to be notified when this happens, since it implies that the EMF will no longer have database access and will become inoperative. Service trackers are often used to detect when services come online or offline, and could similarly be used to track when an EMF service for a given persistence unit becomes available or unavailable.

After retrieving the EMF, it can now be put to use to create the `EntityManager` that we will use to manipulate entities and access data in the database:

```
public class JpaApplication {
    private volatile BundleContext context;
    private volatile EntityManagerFactory emf;

    public void start() {
        if (emf != null) {
            EntityManager em = emf.createEntityManager();

            Contact contact = em.find(Contact.class, 1L);

            if (contact != null) {
                System.out.println(contact);
            } else {
                System.out.println("No contact found.");
            }

            em.close();
        }
    }

    // ...

}
```

Of interest in the code example is that the lookup of the EMF should succeed. This is taken care of in the `Activator`, but when you supply the wrong name for the filter, the service lookup will fail to return a valid EMF. After you successfully obtain the EMF, an `EntityManager` can be created and put to use to do a primary key based lookup of a contact in our database.

Finally, to be able to run the example code, you have to be sure that the manifest includes the following header information:

```
DynamicImport-Package: com.mysql.*
Meta-Persistence: jpa.xml
Include-Resource: jpa.xml=jpa.xml
```

This example bundle is known as an inlined persistent unit. It has a simple application design that makes use of a JPA persistence unit that is co-resident (in the same bundle) with the application code that invokes it. In this design, the application is packaged up into a single bundle, including both the persistence entities and the code that operates on them. Of course, this is not a very modular approach. A more reusable option is to package the persistence unit in a separate bundle and have the application code that needs to operate on the entities have a dependency on the persistence unit bundle or services it offers. An even more advanced design is to nest a persistence unit JAR file inside the persistence bundle. While not common, it does allow a plain JAR containing a persistence unit to be easily incorporated into a bundle. The JAR must be placed on the bundle classpath, and the persistence descriptor must be qualified in the `Meta-Persistence` header using the embedded JAR syntax. For example, if a JAR named *myUnit.jar* contained a *jpa.xml* persistence descriptor in the *META-INF* folder, and the *myUnit.jar* file was placed in the *jpa* folder of the *myBundle.jar* application bundle, the resulting structure is shown in the following hierarchy:

```
myBundle.jar
  jpa/
    myUnit.jar
      META-INF/
        jpa.xml
```

The *MANIFEST.MF* file in the application bundle would then include the following headers:

```
Meta-Persistence: jpa/myUnit.jar!/META-INF/jpa.xml
...
Bundle-ClassPath: ., jpa/myUnit.jar
```

NoSQL

With relational databases reigning supreme in enterprise applications over the last couple of decades, recently a new form of persistence has manifested itself. A number of alternative storage types have been grouped under the name "NoSQL." The rise of non-relational alternatives can be explained by a fundamental shift in architecture that arose from the Web and social media era at the start of the 21st century. The need for scalable clusters of servers and being able to cope with very large amounts of data are the most important drivers.

NoSQL is actually a vaguely defined term. It bears no formal definition and describes a broad range of nonrelational, schema-less, storage alternatives. The meaning of the word NoSQL has different explanations:

- Databases are nonrelational.
- Nonrelational databases don't have the SQL query language.
- Not Only SQL means that we are dealing with a combination of relational and nonrelational storage services.

Whatever it is, NoSQL is not intended to replace the relational database altogether. Relational databases will most definitely still be around in the next decade. The approach of mixing and matching storage services that fit the purpose of the problem to be solved is what is nowadays called *polyglot persistence.*

Polyglot persistence is also becoming more and more popular as the need to use a database as an integration mechanism gets replaced by the use of a higher-level contract exposing well defined interfaces for obtaining data with a business meaning. With Service Oriented Architecture or web-service-based disclosure of information services, the knowledge of how and where the data is stored is hidden behind the service facade, which exposes the data. When the service is responsible for serving the data to the consumer, it can also be responsible for how and where the data is stored and which mechanism is best used to store it.

The power of NoSQL databases comes from two main factors: they are schema-less, and they are designed to scale better than relational databases. Meanwhile, the value of relational databases lies in the fact that they are consistent at all times. Relational databases have been designed for handling concurrency and integration. When dealing with concurrency, the database has to be able to cope with many users looking at the same data and potentially updating it at the same time. In an integration scenario, multiple applications—possibly written in different technologies—can be collaborating on the same set of data. Traditionally, the relational database is very bad at coping with clustering and multiserver environments. There are some tricks to handle this, like sharding or data replication. However, generally speaking, they are unnatural in the relational domain and they come at a price, not only in monetary form (as licenses for such solutions are usually really expensive), but also technically, leading to loss of functionality such as transactions, referential integrity, and querying. Above all, they have a negative impact on the most important feature of the relational database: consistency.

Cloud applications, social networking sites, and large Internet shops nowadays have requirements to handle very large amounts of data, more affectionately known as *web-scale.* These amounts of data can no longer be handled on single server instances. Also, the current datacenter architectures have multiple, cheap server clusters instead of large supercomputers. Both developments add to the fact that relational databases are not the best solution for these problems anymore. Alternative storage solutions, such as NoSQL, should thus be seen as trading off consistency for performance and parallelism.

NoSQL databases can be roughly divided into four categories:

Key/value stores
Popular makes include Redis, Riak, and Memcached

Document stores
Popular makes include CouchDB, and MongoDB

Column-oriented stores
  Popular makes include Cassandra, HBase, and BigTable

Graph databases
  Popular makes include Neo4J

Note that we use the terms store, storage service, and database. The diversity in NoSQL databases leads to a wide variety of ways to store persistent data, ranging from behaving similar to relational databases to giant hashmaps, and some are hardly more than a specific filesystem on disk.

Most if not all NoSQL solutions are schema-less. This means that there is no explicit design of the way in which the data will be stored in the database. Although this may seem strange at first, it provides a great amount of flexibility to application developers. No explicit mapping has to be done between the application and the database to overcome the impedance mismatch as with ORM, leading to less code to write, test, debug, and maintain.

Using schema-less databases makes it a lot easier to dynamically evolve the persistence structure without taking the database and/or the application through the difficult and time-consuming stages of migration.

As a result of loosened requirements for immediate consistency, ACID transactions have gone out of fashion in the NoSQL world. Instead of using ACID, the acronym BASE has arisen as a way of describing the principles of a more optimistic storage strategy. BASE stands for basic availability, soft-state, and eventual consistency. While ACID is a must-have for any relational database, BASE is more of a way of describing the behavior of a generic NoSQL store. No guarantees can be drawn from it. Therefore, when developing against a certain NoSQL solution, you must be intimately familiar with the typical BASE behavior of the chosen solution and work within those constraints. Generally speaking, BASE is defined as:

Basic availability
  The NoSQL storage mechanism appears to work most of the time.

Soft-state
  NoSQL stores don't have to be write-consistent, nor do different replicas have to be mutually consistent all the time.

Eventual consistency
  Stores exhibit consistency at some later point (e.g., lazily at read time).

One particular category of NoSQL databases that goes really well with cloud applications are document stores. In a lot of web applications, communication between the client and the server is largely based upon forms or document-based interaction. Most of the time, this comes down to sending and retrieving JSON structures to and from a RESTful API. In the paragraphs ahead, we will look into interacting with document based databases from a modular application's perspective. To illustrate this, we will provide sample code for *MongoDB*, a very popular make amongst them.

Document Stores

In this chapter, we will explore how to use document stores. Document-oriented databases are designed for storing, retrieving, and managing semistructured data. In contrast to relational databases and their notion of a table, these systems are designed around an abstract notion of a *document*. Document-oriented databases encapsulate data as documents using encodings such as XML, JSON, or some binary encoding formats. Documents inside a document-oriented database are similar to records in relational databases, although the schema-less nature of document-oriented databases imposes fewer limits on the structure of the data inside the document. The next two snippets are both examples of *contacts* stored in the same collection of documents:

```
{
  name:"Paul Bakker",
  phone:"+31987654321"
  email:"paul.bakker.nl@gmail.com"
}

{
  name:"Bert Ertman",
  email:"bert.ertman@gmail.com",
  children:[
    {
      name:"Amber"
      age:4
    }
  ]
}
```

Both documents look alike but have a somewhat different structure. Unlike their relational counterparts, where each record would have the same set of fields and unused fields might be kept empty, there are no empty fields in either document in the document-oriented approach. Document-oriented databases allow for new information to be added to the contents of the document without having to go through the painful stages of a schema change. Information that is left out of a document is not stored as empty fields. This allows for really flexible data structures on the database level. The complexity of dealing with differently structured document is left to layers higher up in the architecture, e.g., your application code.

Using MongoDB as a Document Store

The example code in this chapter uses *MongoDB*. MongoDB is a highly popular NoSQL database, developed by a company called 10gen. MongoDB offers document-oriented storage, full index support, replication and high availability, querying, and map/reduce support, among many other features. This will be a perfect fit for building modular enterprise applications in the cloud.

MongoDB stores structured data as JSON-like documents, using a schema-less approach. In MongoDB, an element of data is called a *document*, and documents are stored in *collections*. One collection may have any number of documents. Any document in a collection can have completely different fields from the other documents. Internally, MongoDB uses a storage format called Binary JSON, or *BSON* for short. BSON is designed to be efficient both in storage space and scan-speed compared to plain JSON. BSON types are considered a superset of JSON types.

Getting Started

Before you can access MongoDB from your application, you have to make sure that you have MongoDB installed on your system. MongoDB itself is written in C++, and there are platform ports available for all the major operating systems, so you shouldn't run into any trouble getting it up and running. It requires hardly any setup, so after downloading it from the Mongo website (*http://bit.ly/17mtASy*), follow the simple setup instructions from the getting started guide, and then you can simply start the mongod service. Default settings will make the MongoDB instance available on localhost, port *27017*.

Create a new Bndtools project in Eclipse, and/or add a new bundle descriptor to contain a new service implementation called service.mongo. For this new service to work properly, we need some MongoDB-related services and a MongoDB Java driver. Furthermore, we need some Jackson bundles to perform the JSON to Mongo (BSON) serialization. Add the following list of dependencies to the build path of the project:

- com.mongodb
- net.vz.mongodb.jackson.mongo-jackson-mapper
- org.amdatu.mongo
- jackson-core-asl
- jackson-mapper-asl

Implementing a Persistent Service

Next, create a new class called MongoAgendaService in a package named agenda.service.mongo. Implement the Agenda interface, and make sure you add the unimplemented methods. In order to interact with Mongo, we can make use of the Amdatu Mongo service component. This component exposes a service called MongoDBService that can be used to interact with Mongo without the hassle of setting up the connection programmatically. For this, we need to declare a dependency to this service:

```
    private volatile MongoDBService mongoDBService;
```

The listConferences method needs to connect to the Mongo database using this service and then look for a collection called conferences. In Mongo terms, a *collection* is roughly comparable to a *table* in a relational database. On the conferences collection, we can do a find in order to retrieve all of its contents. Meanwhile, we have to wrap the output from Mongo with the help of the Jackson mapper. Then we simply iterate over the resulting cursor and return a List of type Conference. If you are not familiar with the Mongo Java API, please use the following code snippet to implement the method listConferences:

```java
public List<Conference> listConferences() {
    DBCollection coll = mongoDBService.getDB().getCollection("conferences");
    JacksonDBCollection<Conference, Object> conferences =
        JacksonDBCollection.wrap(coll, Conference.class);
    DBCursor<Conference> cursor = conferences.find();

    List<Conference> result = new ArrayList<Conference>();
    while (cursor.hasNext()) {
        result.add(cursor.next());
    }

    return result;
}
```

The addConference method also uses the Amdatu MongoDBService to retrieve the conferences collection. It then wraps the conference parameter it receives using Jackson and then saves it into the conferences collection:

```java
public void addConference(Conference conference) {
    DBCollection coll = mongoDBService.getDB().getCollection("conferences");
    JacksonDBCollection<Conference, Object> conferences =
        JacksonDBCollection.wrap(coll, Conference.class);

    conferences.save(conference);
}
```

Next, we need to create an Activator class that makes sure our newly created persistent service implementation gets published. For this, we create another class in the same package. Make sure to extend DependencyActivatorBase and implement its init method. Use the Apache Felix DependencyManager to create a new component. Set the Agenda as its interface and our newly created Mongo service as its implementation class. Since we have a dependency on the Amdatu MongoDBService, we need to list that as well. Make it a required dependency. The result will be something like this:

```java
@Override
public void init(BundleContext ctx, DependencyManager manager)
    throws Exception {

    manager.add(createComponent()
```

```
        .setInterface(Agenda.class.getName(), null)
        .setImplementation(MongoAgendaService.class)
        .add(createServiceDependency()
            .setService(MongoDBService.class)
            .setRequired(true)));
}
```

Open the *service.mongo.bnd* configuration and drag the *agenda.service.mongo* package to the Private Packages. Next, add the `Activator` class. Now switch to the *bnd.bnd* configuration and add the required bundles to the Run Requirements. Resolve and Save the configuration. Since we still have the OSGi container running, our newly deployed bundles have appeared in our runtime automatically. Use the `lb` command to check if all the bundles we need have actually appeared in the runtime. Now use the `listCon ferences` command to see if our new persistent service works.

 You might still get results from the simple `Agenda` implementation that you created in an earlier chapter. In order to have the proper service invoked, either stop the simple `Agenda` implementation explicitly using the `stop` command, or use *service properties* or the *service ranking* mechanism to distinguish between service implementations, as explained in Chapter 3.

From a development perspective, everything seems fine, but when you run the application, it will complain that the `MongoDBService` is unavailable. You can figure this out with the `dm` command in the shell. We did however set up MongoDB on our system and deployed the necessary dependencies in our runtime. Still, the `MongoDBService` was unable to start. How come? This is because the `MongoDBService` needs some mandatory configuration in order to know to what database to connect to. The Amdatu `MongoDB` `Service` uses the Managed Service Factory pattern (see Chapter 4), and in order to bootstrap it, we need to supply a configuration file. In order to supply the configuration file, we need to create a new folder in our *agenda* project. Create a new folder called *load*. This is the default name that the runtime will look for in order to spot configuration files. Next, add an empty text file and call it something like **org.amdatu.mongo-demo.xml**. The configuration file needs at least the following information:

```
dbName=demo
```

For other settings, such as write concerns and read preferences, it assumes some default values. If desired, they can also be overridden using the same configuration file. More information on the various configuration settings can be found in the online documentation of the Amdatu Mongo Service (*http://bit.ly/1dr21ys*). In order for the configuration file to be picked up by the runtime, you need to supply a couple of extra bundles to your Run Requirements in the *bnd.bnd* file:

- `org.apache.felix.configadmin`
- `org.apache.felix.fileinstall`

Resolve, and Save the configuration. Now, lets `lb` again to list all of our bundles. Then run `dm notavail` to check whether there still are some unresolved dependencies. If all is well, we should be all right now. Use the `listConferences` command to list all of the conferences. This should result in an empty list and somehow proves that we are now using the MongoDB database, but unfortunately there is nothing in it yet. One way to get some data in the database is to use the *mongo* shell that comes as part of the MongoDB tools to add a conference like this:

```
> use demo
switched to db demo

> db.conferences.save({"name": "JavaOne", "location": "San Francisco"})
> db.conferences.save({"name": "Devoxx", "location": "Antwerp"})
> db.conferences.save({"name": "Jfokus", "location": "Stockholm"})

> db.conferences.find()
```

By now, our database contains a number of entries. Let's run the `listConferences` command again to check if our service is able to retrieve them.

Oops! We ran into some trouble again. The console now lists an `UnrecognizedProper tyException` claiming that there is a field called `_id` missing in our `Conference` class. This means that there seems to be something wrong with the serialization of the `Con ference` type. There are a couple of ways to solve this, but by far the easiest way is to add a member variable called `_id` to the `Conference` class, as Mongo requires this. Give it a getter and setter as well. Now, run the `listConferences` command again, and everything should work as expected!

Finally, now that your persistent service and Mongo play nice with each other, let's test the `addConference` command as well. Use `listConferences` again to see if the desired result was achieved.

Using the MongoDB Query System

MongoDB has an elaborate query system that allows you to select and filter the documents in a collection along specific fields and values. In the following example, we query for specific documents in the collection by passing a *query document* as a parameter to the `find` method. A query document specifies the criteria the query must match to return a document.

To query for specific conferences by name, you can pass a query document such as `{ name : "JavaOne" }` to the `find` method. MongoDB returns the documents that match these criteria:

```
public List<Conference> findConferencesByName(String name) {
    DBCollection coll = mongoDBService.getDB().getCollection("conferences");
    JacksonDBCollection<Conference, Object> conferences =
        JacksonDBCollection.wrap(coll, Conference.class);

    BasicDBObject query = new BasicDBObject();
    query.put("name", name);
    DBCursor<Conference> cursor = conferences.find(query);

    List<Conference> result = new ArrayList<Conference>();
    while (cursor.hasNext()) {
        result.add(cursor.next());
    }

    return result;
}
```

Taking It Back to the Web

To illustrate how well the document type storage and the Web integrate, let's revisit some of the topics that we covered in Chapter 8 on RESTful Web Services. In that chapter, we discussed the Amdatu Web components and how they provide automatic marshalling of JSON to Java objects, and vice versa. As a result of this, we can now reuse our existing AgendaResource JAX-RS class and look up or add conferences to our MongoDB version of the Agenda implementation:

```
@Path("agenda")
public class AgendaResource {
    private volatile Agenda agendaService;

    @GET
    @Path("conferences")
    @Produces(MediaType.APPLICATION_JSON)
    public List<Conference> listConferences() throws Exception {
        return agendaService.listConferences();
    }

    @POST
    @Path("conferences")
    @Consumes(MediaType.APPLICATION_JSON)
    public void addConference(Conference conference) throws Exception {
        agendaService.addConference(conference);
    }
}
```

To distinguish between the available Agenda implementations, we can use *service properties* as shown in the following example that lists part of the Activator class for the JAX-RS component:

```
@Override
public void init(BundleContext ctx, DependencyManager manager)
    throws Exception {

    manager.add(createComponent()
        .setInterface(Object.class.getName(), null)
        .setImplementation(AgendaResource.class)
        .add(createServiceDependency()
            .setService(Agenda.class, "(persistent=true)")
            .setRequired(true)));
}
```

PART III

Deploying Applications in the Cloud

CHAPTER 10

Deployment

Now that we have seen how to design and build modular applications, we should also know how to actually deploy them to production systems. This book is about building modular cloud apps, so the focus of this chapter will be on deploying to the cloud. We will see, however, that we can use the exact same approach to deploy to in-house servers and even to other types of devices.

Understanding OSGi Runtimes

So far we have been running our code directly from Bndtools, and we have seen a simple example of launching an OSGi container manually from code. How does this apply to production deployments? First we should understand what an OSGi runtime actually is. An OSGi container is the layer on top of the JVM that understands the concept of bundles and implements all the rules and features defined in the OSGi Core Specification. OSGi containers are in general extremely lightweight and are also often used in environments with very constrained resources. In a pure OSGi environment, you might run a bare-bones OSGi container as your deployment platform directly. This works very well, and we will discuss this extensively in this chapter.

An OSGi container can also be embedded in other kinds of server products such as Java EE application servers or even as part of an application. After discussing our preferred deployment model, we will discuss these alternatives.

Choosing an OSGi Framework for Deployment

In all the examples in the book, we have been using Apache Felix. There are several more OSGi implementations, but most of them are closed source. The best known open source alternative to Apache Felix is Eclipse Equinox. Equinox is the OSGi implementation used by the Eclipse IDE. The downside of this is that the development of Equinox has been focused strongly toward Eclipse in the past, which has caused a lot of additional complexity and features that are better left untouched. Although there are plenty of successful examples of applications built on top of Equinox as well, we have a preference toward the Apache Felix framework, that is, unless you are building Eclipse plug-ins.

IaaS versus PaaS versus SaaS

Before talking more about cloud deployments, we should get some definitions straight. When talking about the cloud there are three different categories of cloud that we can talk about:

- IaaS (Infrastructure as a Service)
- PaaS (Platform as a Service)
- SaaS (Software as a Service)

IaaS is about using low-level compute resources in the cloud. Basically you pay for a "server" in the cloud provider's data center. You are responsible yourself to install the server's software, databases, your application bits, etc. This gives you all the freedom you want because you can install whatever you wish on the server. The obvious downside is that you are responsible for all the systems administration and operational maintenance to keep your severs running.

Why is this any different to the traditional model of renting servers? Elasticity is the answer: we can add new servers and terminate servers within minutes. There is no need for long-term contracts or days to weeks of waiting time when ordering a new server. This has some very important benefits: cost reduction, flexibility, and ways to deal with peak load capacity.

When buying or renting servers, it is necessary to be prepared for peak loads; the required server capacity is the maximum capacity that you expect. This is a waste because most applications don't run on their peak capacity 24/7. At night and on weekends, you expect a lot less load. Although the servers are not running peak load 24/7, you are still paying for them. An even bigger problem are unexpected peak loads. What if your website or service suffers a sudden load much higher than the expected peak load capacity? If the servers become unavailable because of the extreme load, it could hurt your business badly. Adding capacity would take at least days in a traditional server environment.

This is where the cloud shines. At any moment, we only have to turn on as much server capacity as we actually need. If the load increases, more capacity is only a few mouse clicks away. That means we only pay for capacity that we actually use, instead of paying for capacity that we might need. Handling extreme loads also becomes a matter of adding more capacity within minutes.

Of course this is all easier said than done. Although the advantages are clear, not every cloud user is automatically making use of this. An application must be prepared for elastic scaling. If our application doesn't scale horizontally, or if it has a component such as a relational database, which is hard to scale, we can't easily add or remove capacity without downtime. Elastic scaling should also be something that should happen automatically, unless you want to manually monitor application usage 24/7.

IaaS gives you all the possibilities of autoscaling and all the freedom on the infrastructural level, but leaves all the (far from trivial) details of actually using this to you. Popular public cloud IaaS offerings include Amazon EC2, Google Compute Engine, and Rackspace Cloud.

Contrary to public cloud is private cloud. This is mostly just a buzzword for something that companies have been doing for a long time already. A private cloud is a virtualized environment within a company's own data center. Virtualization helps achieving the same flexibility as an IaaS provider does; it's easy to start and stop new servers. Of course, this doesn't solve the problem that there should be enough idle hardware available that can be used to start new servers.

Platform as a Service is an offering on a higher level, where you trade flexibility for ease of use. In a PaaS, you only focus on the actual application development; all the infrastructure is taken care of by the service. The exact features and mechanisms vary greatly between providers, but the main concept is that applications are deployed into a managed environment. Most offerings support fully automatic scaling. In theory, this is absolutely great; you write your applications and never ever care about servers, operating systems, and scaling mechanisms. In reality, there is of course a downside to this managed approach, as a managed environment also means a *limited* environment. You can only use what the service provider offers. Often this means whitelisting or blacklisting Java classes, where some classes are not available to the Java Virtual Machine. Most PaaS providers require specific deployment methods and offer only a limited set of supported databases, application servers, and so on. As with everything in software development, this is a trade-off.

Software as a Service is about offering applications as a service over the Internet, as compared to running them from desktop applications like was done in the past. Some well-known examples include Google Docs and Salesforce CRM. The type of cloud applications that we are discussing in this book could very well be SaaS applications, too. If you build applications and make them available in the cloud, you are creating Software as a Service yourself. The architecture and deployment models discussed in this book fit building such services very well.

A Modular PaaS

If we would be looking for a PaaS provider that supports modular OSGi applications, it should support the following:

- An OSGi runtime
- A deployment mechanism that supports modular deployments

At the time of writing, there is no PaaS provider that supports these requirements. Adding support to one of the PaaS platforms for an OSGi container would actually not be that difficult. A modular deployment mechanism is a bigger problem, however. Most PaaS platforms require you to package the whole application in a single deployment package. This could still be used for OSGi applications as well, but we would lose the power to update only a single bundle for incremental updates. This might not be a show stopper for everyone, but after getting used to this, it's hard to give that up.

A reason not to use a PaaS in the first place is vendor lock-in. Besides the limits of class blacklisting and limited data store support, all PaaS vendors offer proprietary APIs for their PaaS services. This means that when you choose to use a PaaS from a specific provider, you tie your application to the specific implementation details of that particular vendor. If for any reason you have to switch to another provider in the future, you will run into some hard-to-overcome problems, i.e., migrating data from one provider to the other.

Fortunately for us, there are some tools in the OSGi space that make it almost trivial to create our own PaaS on top of an IaaS provider, and that's what the rest of this chapter is about.

Apache ACE

Apache ACE is a provisioning server for OSGi. It is used to create distributions from a set of artifacts, i.e., bundles and configuration files, and deploy them to targets such as servers and devices. As shown in Figure 10-1, Apache ACE plays a central role in distributing software artifacts coming from a build server by provisioning them to any number of registered targets. Because Apache ACE understands OSGi versioning semantics, it can also take care of incremental updates to running targets.

With Apache ACE, we solve the deployment/provisioning problem for our custom PaaS environment. This will also play a key role in autoscaling and failover that we will look into a little later. Let's start by setting up Apache ACE.

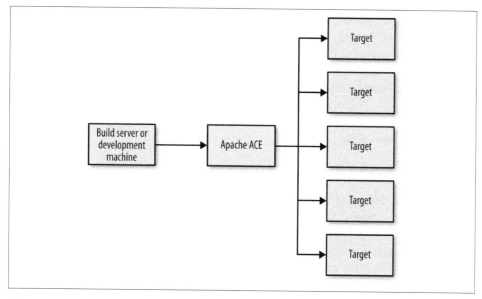

Figure 10-1. Apache ACE provisioning software distributions to registered targets

Installing Apache ACE

Apache ACE can be installed almost everywhere; all we need is a Java Virtual Machine, which is quite ubiquitous nowadays. When working with Apache ACE, we can either use the web user interface, or its RESTful Web Service API. When using Apache ACE to provision cloud servers, it makes sense to install Apache ACE on a cloud node as well, but technically speaking, it really doesn't matter where Apache ACE runs.

Start by downloading the latest binary release from *http://ace.apache.org*. Extract the downloaded archive and enter the *server-allinone* folder. Now start the Apache ACE server by running the JAR file:

```
java -jar server-allinone.jar
```

Apache ACE will start on port 8080 by default, so make sure this port is available. Open a web browser and go to *http://localhost:8080/ace* (or the hostname your server is listening on).

You should now see the Apache ACE web user interface. It shows four different (still empty) columns: `artifacts`, `features`, `distributions`, and `targets`. The `artifacts` column will contain all the individual artifacts such as bundles and configuration files. Artifacts can be grouped into *features*, and features can be grouped into *distributions*. Finally, a distribution is assigned to *targets*.

So what is a target exactly? A target is any OSGi framework with the Apache ACE management agent installed. The management agent is an OSGi bundle that calls back to the Apache ACE server and takes care of deployments and updates to the target. Because the management agent is just an OSGi bundle, we can make almost everything a target. A server that runs an OSGi framework can be a target, embedded devices that run OSGi can be targets, Java EE application servers with an embedded OSGi container can be targets, etc. Although the focus of this book is on cloud applications (and deployments), it should be clear that you can use the same tools to provision any other kind of deployment scenario.

Starting Deployment Targets

Before diving into autoscaling and starting targets automatically, we should know how to start a target manually. As discussed, a target is basically any OSGi container with the management agent bundle installed. To make things even easier, the Apache ACE project has a launcher available that contains the Apache Felix framework with the management agent installed. This is exactly what we need for cloud deployments. Find the *ace-launcher.jar* and start it with the following command:

```
java -jar ace-launcher.jar identification=target-id
discovery=http://localhost:8080
```

This will start the Apache Felix container and a management agent that will register itself with its `target-id` on the Apache ACE server listening on *http://localhost:8080*. That's it! Now we can start to deploy some bundles.

Creating a Deployment

In order to create a deployment, we need to start by uploading some bundles to Apache ACE. For this, we need the ACE web UI open in a browser. If the target is still running, you should see it listed in the `targets` column. Now click the "Add artifact" button to upload some bundles. A dialog will appear. Simply drag some bundle JAR files from the filesystem to the dialog, and they will be uploaded. For experimental purposes, it's best to start with a small set of bundles, for example, only the Gogo shell bundles.

When the uploading has completed, the names of the files are listed in the dialog. Close the dialog by clicking the Add button. The bundles should now be listed in the `arti facts` column. Now create a feature by clicking the "Add feature" button, and give it a name (e.g., `shell`). Now select all bundles in the `artifacts` column and drag them on top off the feature you just created. The artifacts are now linked to this feature. Repeat these steps to create a distribution.

Now drag the distribution to the target and click Save. If the Gogo shell is part of the deployment, you should immediately see a shell appear on the target. Deployment completed! You can play around with the deployment by adding some more bundles or by removing bundles. After hitting the Save button, the target should reflect the changes almost instantly.

Resetting Apache ACE

When playing around with Apache ACE, it is sometimes desirable to just start over with a clean sheet and remove all artifacts, features, and distributions. This can be done by removing the *felix* directory and removing all *artifact-** files from the *store* directory. Restart Apache ACE, and everything is back to a clean installation.

The same can be done with a target. Stop that target and remove the *felix-cache* directory. Start the client again, and it will be provisioned cleanly with the latest available deployment package.

Incremental Updates

You might be wondering what exactly is the benefit of modular deployments if we still have to create a distribution that logically contains all separate bundles. The benefit comes after the initial deployment, when we want to update parts of the system. First of all, we can add new features to a distribution any time we want. Updating existing bundles is even more interesting.

Apache ACE understands the `major.minor.micro.qualifier` versioning scheme used by OSGi. When a new bundle is uploaded with a symbolic name that already exists, but with a higher version, Apache ACE will automatically remove the old version from the deployment and replace it with the new one. As soon as you click Save, all targets that contain this bundle will be updated. Apache ACE is also smart about creating deployment packages; it will only send those artifacts to the client that are actually changed.

The benefit of modular deployments now becomes clear. We can update single bundles and push them to a large number of targets within seconds. There is no need to create a large, all-containing WAR or EAR file just to update a single bundle. And as an extra benefit, because of service dynamics, there is usually also no reason to stop the application while updating (smaller) parts of it.

Deploying Configuration

You might have noticed that in Apache ACE we talk about artifacts instead of bundles. This implies that there are other types of deployable artifacts than just bundles. Theoretically speaking, we can deploy any kind of file as long as we implement a so-called *resource processor*. A resource processor is an OSGi service that implements the standardized `ResourceProcessor` interface, which is part of the Deployment Admin specification.

For configuration files, a resource processor is already available. Configuration files in the MetaType standard can be deployed out of the box. There is one minor step to take; we need to add the `AutoConf Resource Processor` bundle. Click the "Add artifact" button in Apache ACE again and you should find the `AutoConf bundle` in the top part of the dialog. After adding `AutoConf`, we can add configuration files by uploading them just like bundles.

Parameterized Configuration

We can take configuration even a step further by making configuration parameterized. Configuration files are automatically preprocessed as Velocity templates by Apache ACE. We can add variables in the configuration files that will be replaced before sending the file to a target as part of a deployment package. The actual values of the variables can be configured in the Apache ACE UI by double-clicking a target. A dialog will appear with information about the target. Click the Tag Editor tab and enter custom variables as key/value pairs.

This mechanism is extremely useful when working with the same deployment for different environments, where each environment works with a different database, for example.

Solving Deployment Issues

Sooner or later you might run into issues with a deployment. In most cases, they are obvious, e.g., resolver errors, but in some cases, Apache ACE is not able to install anything at all. In that case, there are some handy steps that can be taken to track down the problem.

Start by restarting the target without removing the *felix-cache* folder first. If there is an error with AutoConf or your configuration files, the error may become visible while starting the framework. If this didn't solve the problem, it is always good to restart the target with a fresh deployment by removing the *felix-cache*. Check if a deployment package is being installed by checking if the *felix-cache* folder is being filled up. If this is not the case, there is no deployment package for the target, which may point to a configuration mistake in Apache ACE.

Another very useful debugging tool is running a target locally. Remember that you can start a target from wherever you can connect to the Apache ACE server. Start with a small set of bundles, and extend the deployment step by step to find the source of the error.

Configuring the Apache ACE Launcher

The Apache ACE launcher can be configured with framework options and Java Virtual Machine options. Configuring framework options is sometimes required when some extra system or bootstrap classes need to be loaded. For example, we can load the sun.* and com.sun.* classes, which are normally not exported by the OSGi framework:

```
java -jar ace-launcher.jar
fwOption=org.osgi.framework.bootdelegation=sun.*,com.sun.*
identification=example discovery=http://localhost:8080
```

Another useful property is the refresh interval that the management agent will use to check the Apache ACE server for new updates. By default, this is two seconds, which is unnecessarily short for most production use cases. You could, for example, set the refresh interval to a minute by adding the following parameter:

```
-Drefreshinterval=60000
```

We can also pass Java Virtual Machine parameters in the same way. For most production systems, it's a best practice to explicitly set memory settings, for example. Using the ACE Launcher, this can be done by simply passing them as VM parameters using the -D notation. The correct settings vary greatly between deployment systems and applications, of course, so do not take these example numbers as any kind of reference:

```
-DXmx:1000m -DXms:512m -XX:MaxPermSize=200m
```

Autoscaling

Now that we can manually start Apache ACE targets and deploy our software, it's time to take a look at autoscaling. As discussed in the introduction of this chapter, autoscaling is one of the most important reasons to move to the cloud. A typical cloud application deployment view is shown in Figure 10-2. The figure shows a load balancer that acts as the key component of our infrastructure and a number a nodes, representing server instances, divided into several availability zones. The latter provides us with the ability to spread the load over multiple datacenters of the IaaS provider, reducing the risk of a single datacenter outage.

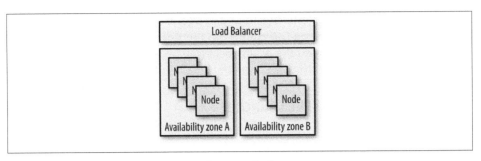

Figure 10-2. Deployment view for multi-zone deployment

A horizontally scalable architecture is key for autoscaling because it allows adding and removing nodes at will. We start with a load balancer, and each node will be registered to that load balancer. As soon as a new node is registered with the load balancer, it will start directing requests to that node. Besides the autoscalable nodes that run the OSGi software, we might also use some components that are not automatically scalable such as a database.

Disposable Nodes

With the autoscaling model, we can add nodes to the cluster by simply starting them. This offers another interesting advantage that we like to call *disposable nodes*. Nodes in a cluster don't have state and are exactly the same as any other node in the autoscaling cluster. Because nodes can be so easily installed, we can also very easily replace them.

When a node starts to misbehave, either because of a hardware or software malfunction, we simply replace the node with a new one. This is what we mean with *disposable*. When a node is unhealthy, just turn it off and start a new one. We don't need to maintain running nodes; we just replace them.

Because of this, the cluster even becomes self-healing. When the load balancer finds a node unhealthy, it can just replace it with a new one.

Now we need some automated mechanism to start and stop nodes, provision them with software, and register them to the load balancer. Unfortunately, there are no cloud agnostic tools or APIs yet to do so. JClouds (*http://bit.ly/154iU91*) is a nice Java library to start, stop, and configure nodes on different cloud providers, but it doesn't deal with provisioning and more advanced (often cloud-specific) configuration. Therefore we will need some cloud specific setup. For the example, we will use Amazon EC2.

Start by creating a load balancer on Amazon EC2. This can easily be done using the EC2 web console. We do not add nodes to the load balancer manually, so for the moment, the load balancer doesn't do anything yet.

Next download, install, and configure *Amazon AutoScaling* tools. This is a set of console commands that can be used to configure autoscaling. With AutoScaling, we can automatically start nodes. However, when a node is started, we still need a mechanism that registers the node to our Apache ACE server for provisioning. To do so, we create a custom machine image (or *AMI* in Amazon EC2 terms). We generally use a standard Linux image as a basis.

First of all, the image needs a Java runtime and Groovy (because the startup script example is in Groovy), so both need to be installed. Now we need the Apache ACE launcher JAR file and a boot script that starts up the Apache ACE launcher. To make the image as flexible as possible, it should be able to configure things like the Apache ACE server URL and its *target ID* externally. Amazon AutoScaling has the concept of *user data* for that. When configuring a cluster, we can specify this data, and from the node, we can access this data using a HTTP API.

Taking these things into consideration, we have two startup scripts: a bash script that takes care of starting the ACE launcher, and a Groovy script that fetches the user data and does the registration to the Apache ACE server. User data becomes available for a target on *http://169.254.169.254/latest/user-data*. This is a special address that Amazon makes available to nodes and is only accessible by the node itself. From there, we fetch the aceUrl and save it to a file *discovery.txt* for later use. We then use the Apache ACE REST API to register the node as a target. Details about the REST API can be found on the Apache ACE website. As an example, we also fetch a user data property domain and set this as a *tag* on the ACE target. We should be able to see and change that property from the Apache ACE UI after registration:

```groovy
import groovyx.net.http.HTTPBuilder
import static groovyx.net.http.ContentType.*
import static groovyx.net.http.Method.*
import java.util.concurrent.TimeUnit

@Grab(group = 'org.codehaus.groovy.modules.http-builder',
    module = 'http-builder', version = '0.5.2')
def url = 'http://my.ace.server:8080'

// Amazon AutoScaling user data becomes available on this url
def httpUserData = new groovyx.net.http.HTTPBuilder('http://169.254.169.254')
def userData = [:]

httpUserData.get(path: 'latest/user-data') {userDataResp, reader ->
    reader.text.eachLine { line ->
        def values = line.split("=")
        userData[values[0]] = values[1]
    }

    if (userData['aceUrl']) {
        url = userData['aceUrl'];
    }
```

```
def discoveryfile = new File("discovery.txt")
discoveryfile << url

def http = new groovyx.net.http.HTTPBuilder(url)
def httpCreateTarget = new groovyx.net.http.HTTPBuilder(url)
def httpCreateDistribution2Target = new groovyx.net.http.HTTPBuilder(url)
def httpCommit = new groovyx.net.http.HTTPBuilder(url)

def createWS = http.post(path: 'client/work') {resp ->
    def location = resp.headers['Location'].toString() - 'Location: '
    def targetName = userData['targetprefix'] + '-' +
        System.currentTimeMillis()
    def nodeidfile = new File("nodeid.txt")
    nodeidfile << targetName
    httpCreateTarget.request(POST, JSON) {
        uri.path = "$location/target"
        body = [attributes: [id: targetName, autoapprove: true],
            tags: ['domain': userData['domain']]]
        response.success = {
            httpCreateDistribution2Target.request(POST, JSON) {
                uri.path = "$location/distribution2target"

                def leftEndpoint = '(name=' + userData['targetprefix'] + ')'
                def rightEndpoint = '(id=' + targetName + ')'
                body = [attributes: [leftEndpoint: leftEndpoint,
                    rightEndpoint: rightEndpoint,
                    leftCardinality: 1, rightCardinality: 1]]
                response.success = {
                    httpCommit.post(path: location) {
                        def completedFile = new File("completed")
                        completedFile << "completed"
                    }
                }
            }
        }
    }
}
```

The bash script doesn't do more than start the Groovy script and start the Apache ACE launcher upon completion. The launcher is started in a *screen* so that we always log into a node using SSH and work with the OSGi shell directly. Of course, you should set memory settings for the launcher appropriate for the application you will be deploying or set this automatically depending on the node type:

```
groovy /home/ec2-user/install.groovy >> /var/log/example
echo "Now waiting for completed file" >> /var/log/example
while [ ! -f /home/ec2-user/completed ]
do
  sleep 2
done
```

```
screen -dmS acetarget java -jar ace-launcher.jar identification=`cat nodeid.txt`
discovery=`cat discovery.txt`
```

Make sure the bash script is executed upon booting the image. For most Linux systems, you can put the script in */etc/rc.d/rc.local*.

Now we have taken the last step in configuring the AutoScaling itself. Use the following two console commands to configure a cluster:

```
./as-create-launch-config example --image-id yourami --instance-type m1.small
--region eu-west-1 --group your-sg --user-data-file example-userdata.txt
./as-create-auto-scaling-group example --launch-configuration example
--minsize 1 --max-size 3 --availability-zones eu-west-1a --load-balancers mylb
--tag "k=Name,v=mycluster,p=true"
```

This creates a cluster with one node that will immediately be started. If your AMI boot script is set up correctly, you should see the new target in Apache ACE within a few minutes. AutoScaling takes care of registering the node to the load balancer.

If this works correctly, we can start playing with automatically adding and removing nodes. Amazon AutoScaling has all kind of triggers available that can be used for this. In a scenario where we have a steady load pattern (e.g., busy during office hours, quiet at night), a scheduled trigger can be very useful.

The following example scales up to three nodes at 8 a.m. and scales down to one node at 6 p.m.:

```
./as-put-scheduled-update-group-action example-scale-up --recurrence "0 8 * * *"
--desired-capacity 3 --auto-scaling-group example

./as-put-scheduled-update-group-action example-scale-up
--recurrence "0 18 * * *" --desired-capacity 1 --auto-scaling-group example
```

So what did we create exactly? Figure 10-3 is the setup that is running now.

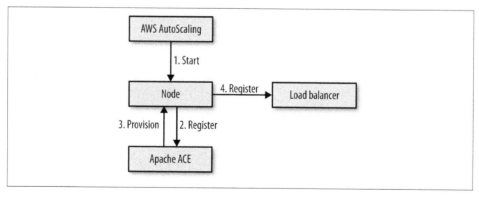

Figure 10-3. Autoscaling setup using AWS AutoScaling and Apache ACE

As discussed earlier, it is currently not possible to do this in a cloud-vendor-independent way. On the other hand, this is only the scaling and load balancing configuration. Our application, and the way we do provisioning, needs no change when moving to another cloud. Our example used the Amazon EC2 specific way of configuring this, but similar results can be achieved using other public IaaS providers' technology. Currently, there is a research effort going on that's investigating a cloud agnostic way of doing this, and concrete results will be developed into the Amdatu project. Enterprise OSGi RFC 183 will make this easier as well. However, this is currently all work in progress but could be very interesting movements to make OSGi in the cloud even easier.

CHAPTER 11

Alternative Deployment Methods

In the previous chapter, we discussed how to deploy modular applications in the cloud, including how to deal with cloud capabilities such as autoscaling and failover. Although we strongly believe this is the future of deployments, we also recognize that this might not be feasible for everyone. Company politics or legislation can require deployments on specific platforms and existing infrastructure. OSGi applications can be deployed in many ways, however, and we will discuss some of them in this chapter to give you some alternatives to consider.

You might also be wondering if using an OSGi container directly is not a little too bare bones. What about clustering, management, and failover? Instead, Java EE application servers have a rich set of features in the area of management consoles and administration features. Would it be worth using an application server like this? Most modern Java EE application servers support OSGi to some extent. There are even application servers specifically created for deploying OSGi applications. Why choose one over the other?

Whether it makes sense to choose an application server as your deployment platform really depends on your deployment model. For the production applications that we have been developing and deploying into the cloud, we used nothing but bare-bones Apache Felix runtimes. We very much support the idea of disposable runtimes, where you can simply replace a node completely on full deployments. As we have discussed in Chapter 10, we can easily accomplish this when using a provisioning server such as Apache ACE. There are several advantages to this approach, but it also comes with limitations. The advantages include the following:

- No overhead or application server memory footprint.
- Easy to scale; the nodes are extremely lightweight.
- No management; if a node becomes problematic, we simply replace it.

Although modern Java EE application servers are quite lightweight, they are still a lot heavier than a plain Apache Felix framework, for example. In server environments, this doesn't matter that much, but it's still a waste. More important, they often require more installation and configuration. Again, this might not be a huge problem, but it's not optimal either.

There are limitations that might be a problem for more traditional deployments, however:

- No clustering at the application server level.
- No "bundled" deployments.
- No management console.
- Only one application can be installed per framework.

The model where nodes are provisioned by a provisioning server and run in the cloud, *the disposable node model*, works very well. If the architecture is also horizontally scalable, there is really no reason to depend on the application server for clustering and management. This approach is very different from the more traditional deployment model that most application servers use. Traditionally, a single application server is used to host multiple applications. One of the reasons to do this is to save the memory footprint overhead of the application server itself. Another reason is that nonvirtualized server environments are more difficult to manage when multiple application servers are installed on a single machine. This makes it much more difficult to do maintenance on applications, because the applications are never truly isolated from one another. Some application servers offer multidomain setups where each application server domain is somewhat isolated, but the applications are still running in the same application server. Taking the application server down will take all applications down as well.

Dealing with a single application per server makes this a lot easier. When moving to the cloud, this all feels very outdated, and if you are moving to the cloud (or a virtualized environment in general), you should be considering getting rid of the application server altogether.

If you are not in this position, or work in an environment where management decides on the application server to use (trust us, we have been there), you might still be looking for alternatives. We discuss several alternatives in the next sections.

Packaging an Application as an Executable JAR

Bndtools has a feature that makes it possible to run OSGi applications anywhere Java is installed without any extra requirements. Bndtools can export a complete application to a single executable JAR file. This JAR file contains the OSGi framework and all bundles that are part of the application. When the JAR is started, the framework is installed, and the bundles are deployed in the framework. The JAR is self-contained and doesn't require anything besides Java.

To export a run configuration to an executable JAR, you open a run configuration file in Bndtools. Near the buttons to start and debug the run configuration, there is also the export button.

It's easy to imagine the flexibility this offers. Deploying to a server that doesn't "support" OSGi is as simple as uploading and starting the JAR file. Of course, this doesn't support advanced features such as modular updates to the running application, but these may not be needed in every case. This kind of deployment also makes it possible to integrate with some of the PaaS providers available today. One example of this is the RedHat OpenShift PaaS platform. With OpenShift, you can deploy custom application runtimes by checking in the binaries in Git. Next you would have to write a startup script that starts up the application on a cloud node (or *Gear*, as they call it). This way of deployment can be used for any kind of server platform, but simply starting a JAR file doesn't require any extra downloads (faster deployments), and the startup script is trivial.

Application Servers

In this section, we will discuss several application servers that can be used to deploy OSGi applications onto.

Oracle GlassFish Application Server

Internally, the GlassFish application server is completely built on top of OSGi. Technically speaking, GlassFish is an Apache Felix runtime with a whole bunch of bundles preinstalled. Most GlassFish users will probably never notice this fact, because they deploy WAR and EAR files containing traditional, nonmodular, Java EE applications. GlassFish does make it possible to work with OSGi bundles directly, and even adds some very useful features. GlassFish offers several ways to deploy OSGi bundles. You can install bundles using the administrative UI, the command line, or using the built-in Apache Felix File Install features. The domain folder in a GlassFish installation contains an *autodeploy/bundles* folder. Simply drop your bundles into this folder, and they will be installed in GlassFish automatically.

Using Apache ACE to provision GlassFish

We have already seen that file based deployments are not ideal. Because GlassFish can be considered an OSGi framework, you can also install the Apache ACE Management Agent bundle in GlassFish. This way, you make GlassFish a target that can be provisioned by Apache ACE. All that is required is some trivial setup:

1. Download the Apache ACE Management Agent bundle.

2. Install the bundle in GlassFish by adding it to the *GlassFish/domains/domain1/autodeploy/bundles* folder.

3. Start GlassFish and open the management console (*http://localhost:4848*).

4. Open Configurations → System Properties and add the following two properties: `identification` and `discovery`.

5. Restart GlassFish.

The `identification` and `discovery` system properties are required to configure the Management Agent with an identifier for the `target` and the URL of your Apache ACE server (See Chapter 10).

After restarting GlassFish, it should be registered to the Apache ACE server. You can now install and update bundles the usual way using Apache ACE.

Using the OSGi shell

GlassFish also comes with an OSGi shell out of the box, which can be accessed remotely using Telnet. For security purposes, this is disabled by default. Open the *GlassFish/config/osgi.properties* files and change the `glassfish.osgi.start.level.final` property from **2** to **3**. GlassFish uses start levels to enable certain features, and the remote OSGi shell is only started in the highest start level. The shell should now be available on port *6666*:

```
telnet localhost 6666
```

Interacting with GlassFish Java EE APIs

The real compelling feature of the GlassFish application server is that it exposes a lot of the Java EE APIs to OSGi bundles. This means you can use EJBs with declarative transaction management and JPA integration. Although transactions and JPA are available in a pure OSGi environment, using, for example, EclipseLink or OpenJPA, integration with EJB makes this a lot easier.

EJB and JPA

To illustrate interacting with EJB and JPA from an OSGi bundle, we first create a simple example EJB like this:

```
@Stateless
public class ExampleEJB implements ExampleComponent {

    @PersistenceContext EntityManager em;
    public void savePerson(String name) {
        em.persist(new Person(name));
    }

    public List<String> listPersonNames() {
```

```
        return em.createQuery("select p.name from Person p", String.class)
            .getResultList();
    }
}
```

In the example, we inject a JPA `EntityManager` using the `@PersistenceContext` annotation. This annotation is part of the EJB/JPA integration as defined in Java EE. Because this is a Stateless Session Bean, we also get transactions for free; a transaction is started and committed at each method call.

To use JPA, we have to configure a *persistence.xml*. This is done exactly the same way as you would do it in a normal Java EE application:

```
<?xml version="1.0" encoding="UTF-8"?>
<persistence xmlns:xsi="http://www.w3.org/2001/XMLSchema-instance"
    xsi:schemaLocation="http://java.sun.com/xml/ns/persistence
    http://java.sun.com/xml/ns/persistence/persistence_2_0.xsd"
    version="2.0" xmlns="http://java.sun.com/xml/ns/persistence">
    <persistence-unit name="myPU">
        <jta-data-source>jdbc/__default</jta-data-source>
        <properties>
            <property name="eclipselink.ddl-generation" value="create-tables"/>
            <property name="eclipselink.ddl-generation.output-mode"
                value="database"/>
        </properties>
    </persistence-unit>
</persistence>
```

The *persistence.xml* file must be present in the *META-INF* folder. We can use a BND instruction to do so. In this example, the file is stored in the *persistence* folder in our project:

```
Include-Resource: META-INF=persistence
```

That's it; you should be able to deploy this as a bundle (e.g., using Apache ACE) in GlassFish, assuming that GlassFish's built-in database is running.

Another nice feature of EJBs in GlassFish is that we can export Stateless Session Beans as OSGi services. Other OSGi services can invoke this service without even knowing that actually an EJB is invoked. For this, we need one extra header in our manifest:

```
Export-EJB: ALL
```

The header can either be used to export *all* EJBs, or a narrowed-down list of fully qualified class names. Note that Stateful Session Beans are not supported to be exported as OSGi services. The reason for this is that the OSGi services model doesn't have the notion of "client" specific instances of services.

Now that we have it exported, another OSGi service can start to use an EJB as if it were a normal OSGi service:

```
public class Activator extends DependencyActivatorBase {

    @Override
    public synchronized void init(BundleContext context,
        DependencyManager manager) throws Exception {
        manager.add(createComponent()
            .setImplementation(EJBClient.class)
            .add(createServiceDependency()
                .setService(ExampleEJB.class)
                .setRequired(true))
        );
    }

    @Override
    public synchronized void destroy(BundleContext context,
        DependencyManager manager) throws Exception {
    }
}

public class EJBClient {
    private volatile ExampleEJB bean;

    public void start() {
        bean.savePerson("Some new person");
        List<String> listPersonNames = bean.listPersonNames();
        for (String name : listPersonNames) {
            System.out.println(name);
        }
    }
}
```

EJB support is in the process of being standardized by the OSGi Enterprise Expert Group. The current direction for the specification has a very similar model as the current (nonstandardized) experimental support in GlassFish. The final specification is scheduled for R6.

Web Application Bundles and JAX-RS

Another nice feature in GlassFish is support for JAX-RS and Web Application Bundles. Web Application Bundles are discussed in Chapter 8. Although this is available in pure OSGi environments as well, the GlassFish way is very similar to normal Java EE development. With these features, GlassFish can be a convenient transitioning path from traditional Java EE to OSGi.

GlassFish versus a plain OSGi container

Since GlassFish is technically just a very advanced OSGi container, you could be wondering if GlassFish is not a much better alternative to a plain OSGi container where you build up your full stack yourself. This strongly depends on your goals and background. Although GlassFish tries to bridge the gap between Java EE and OSGi, it only succeeds in this partly. Yes, you can deploy OSGi bundles and services and mix code with Java EE code, but in practice, this involves some mechanisms such as classpath scanning that

---

are considered bad practices in OSGi. These mechanisms hurt the dynamic behavior of services and make it more difficult to unlock the full potential of OSGi.

At the same time, you can create a pure OSGi stack, a la carte, with a lot of the same APIs using components from the Amdatu project, for example, without sacrificing service dynamics. If you are planning to build a new application, we strongly advise trying the pure OSGi way. Although some Java EE technologies such as EJB and JSF are not available, you should ask yourself if you really need those in the first place.

If you are in the process of migrating a Java EE application to a more modular approach using OSGi, GlassFish might be the perfect place to start. Your old code will still be working while you can start building OSGi services.

RedHat JBoss Application Server

The JBoss Application Server is not built on OSGi. Instead, it is built on top of JBoss Modules, which is the home-cooked modularity system of RedHat. Because JBoss Modules is not a full alternative to OSGi, the application server also offers an OSGi container on top of this. Similar to GlassFish, it offers some additional features, such as Web Application Bundle support. It does not offer support for using EJB and JPA from OSGi bundles yet, which makes the gap between Java EE and OSGi components in an application quite large.

It is possible to inject OSGi services into Java EE components such as servlets, but this way, you will lose many of the benefits of dynamic services. Mixed Java EE and OSGi components still have the benefit of more modular deployments, but this is only a small part of why you should be looking at OSGi.

IBM WebSphere® Application Server

IBM WebSphere Application Server has the same goal as GlassFish in that it makes mixing Java EE and OSGi easy. WebSphere and the tooling around WebSphere have features to deal with libraries and different versions of libraries more easily compared to the traditional hierarchical classloading mechanism in Java EE. Similar to GlassFish, these features are very useful if you are still stuck with large amounts of existing Java EE code and can't move to a pure OSGi environment yet. Having support for OSGi in an application server makes this process easier, and you can at least have some of the benefits of OSGi without migrating all your code. WebSphere includes support for JPA and Web Bundle Archives and will have early support for EJB when the specification matures.

Apache Karaf

Apache Karaf is very different from the application servers discussed so far. While GlassFish, JBoss Application Server, and IBM WebSphere find their roots in Java EE, Apache Karaf is an application server focused entirely on OSGi. Karaf tries to add some enterprise features on top of a plain OSGi environment, such as more advanced deployment features, a management shell, and integration with messaging systems. Although some features, such as the shell, are compelling, there are a lot of features that are focused on integration strategies of nonmodular applications. These might be very helpful while transitioning from other environments, but shouldn't be used when developing new applications in our opinion. Apache Karaf certainly has its place, but is not required when building applications the way we have discussed in this book.

Eclipse Virgo

Eclipse Virgo is similar to Apache Karaf in the sense that it was designed as an OSGi container with enterprise features, without having roots in Java EE. Virgo was donated to Eclipse by VmWare and has its origins in the defunct Spring DM Server. Virgo has a strong focus on using the Spring framework in OSGi applications and offers a deployment model which is similar to traditional Spring framework deployments. It can also host multiple applications in a single server. Just as with Apache Karaf, we do not advise using it, because it adds overhead and complexity that we do not need. If you are migrating from a Spring framework environment toward OSGi, Virgo might offer a more gradual migration path.

Example Application

This appendix describes an example application that serves as a reference application for most of the technologies that we have discussed in this book. All the code of the example application can be found in an online repository.

Introduction

The example application is a web shop. It contains an end user frontend where a customer can browse, search, and order products. It also contains an administrative backend where products and orders can be managed. The application is built on the stack described in this book. Although the application is relatively small, it is a realistic view of a modular, service-based, web application. If the application were larger, the architecture would be exactly the same; there would just be more bundles with more services.

Finding and Running the Source Code

Books are a bad way to list large amounts code. An IDE is much better at this, so we decided to put all the code in an online repository. You can simply check out the code and import it in an Bndtools workspace. The sources are in a Git repository, so make sure you have Git installed. From the command line, you can check out the code as follows:

```
git clone https://bitbucket.org/amdatu/showcase/
```

Create a new Bndtools workspace and choose Import → Existing Projects and select all projects in the directory that you just cloned from Git.

You can run the code using the `webshop.bndrun` configuration in the "run" project. The example uses MongoDB, so you need to install and run a Mongo installation. The database name is `webshop`.

When the application is started, you can use both the customer-facing frontend and the administrative backend.

```
Customer front-end: http://localhost:8080
Administrative back-end: http://localhost:8080/admin
```

The login for the administrative backend is *admin / admin*.

Layered View

There are multiple ways we can look at the architecture. The first high-level view is the technology stack in a layered view as depicted in Figure A-1.

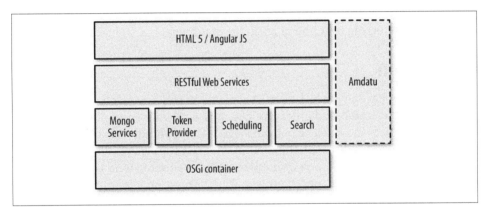

Figure A-1. Layered view

The user interface is entirely based on AngularJS. In fact, we could have used any JavaScript framework, and learning this particular framework is not really in the scope of this book. However, we will discuss how we applied modularity in the user interface.

All interaction between the AngularJS client and the backend is REST based. Amdatu Web is used to implement the RESTful resources using JAX-RS. Authentication and authorization in the RESTful web services is implemented using a custom authentication mechanism on top of Amdatu Security, which will be discussed later in the appendix.

The RESTful web services are just a thin layer on top of OSGi services that provide the bulk of the code. The services implement data storage on top of MongoDB and full-text search with Solr.

Component View

So far, Figure A-1 doesn't tell much about modularity yet. For that we have to zoom in a little bit more. First we will look at the exported APIs and how the different services correlate as described in Figure A-2.

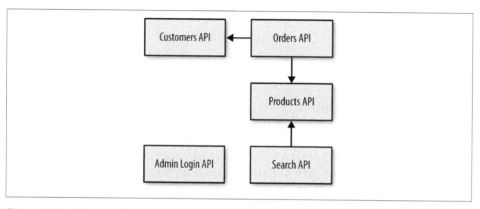

Figure A-2. API correlation

The API bundles contain both domain classes shared by services, and service interfaces. Some APIs depend on other APIs. For example, the Order domain class contains a Customer. Both classes are in different API bundles. This way other services can use Customer as well, without dragging in things they don't need such as Order. Cyclic dependencies should be avoided at all times; there are design patterns to help with this.

Zooming in even more, we can see services and dependencies between services as shown in Figure A-3. Of course, the services only know about the exported APIs of the services they consume and not about the service implementations. Remember that the RESTful resources are OSGi services as well. We can see that services can use (multiple) other services to combine them to provide new functionality.

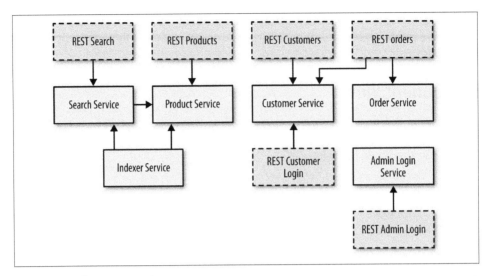

Figure A-3. Component view

In a larger application, there are often some services, sometimes called "core services," that are used by many other services to be combined for different kinds of functionality. This is reusability at its best. To make services reusable, they should do only one thing. For example, the Customer Service in the application only persists customers. Customer related functionality is implemented in other services, like Order Service and Login.

Development View

When working with small services that only do a single thing, you quickly end up with a large number of bundles. To structure this during development, you can use sub-bundles in Bndtools. Basically this comes down to generating multiple bundles from a single Bndtools project. This still keeps our modular approach intact, because we still generate the same bundles with the same visibility rules, but it makes development easier by grouping bundles together.

Most of the time, we group bundles that are closely related. For example, the *customer* project contains four bundles:

- `customer.api`
- `customer.login.rest`
- `customer.rest`
- `customer.mongo`

This contains all the layers of a part of our domain and is a convenient grouping in general. Remember that the Bundle-SymbolicName of the generated bundles is derived from the project name, so this is already an indication of whether bundles should be in the same project or not.

Modularized Frontend

The frontend of the example application is built in HTML 5 using AngularJS. Using client-side technology, we move a large part of the code to JavaScript. Putting large amounts of JavaScript together without some way of modularization would create the same maintenance problems as it would on the server side. Therefore, we choose to separate the UI in different bundles. Technically those bundles contain completely independent applications, but this is invisible for an end user. Each application listens on a separate URL.

The example application's UI is packaged in four separate bundles:

- webshop.admin.general.ui
- webshop.admin.orders.ui
- webshop.admin.products.ui
- webshop.frontend.ui

The end user's frontend is small enough to be packaged in a single bundle, which contains a single AngularJS application. The administration side of the example application is separated by feature; the administration of orders and the management of prod ucts is completely separated. The different parts of the application are integrated together by providing some resources, like the menu bar, from a bundle containing shared resources.

The shared resources bundle has knowledge about all the other functional parts of the application; if a new application bundle were to be added, the menu bar in the shared resources bundle would have to be changed manually. We could make this more dynamic by adding a RESTful resource that lists the URLs for all registered UI bundles, for example.

Note that we modularized the UI by choosing a different packaging strategy; we didn't actually change anything in the UI code. The UI itself is implemented using a typical AngularJS setup. The application doesn't have any server-side session state at all. All necessary state is kept on the client and is easy to scale horizontally.

The UI code is made available to users using the Amdatu Resource Handler, which can serve resources from folders within a bundle.

The application uses a servlet filter to redirect users from the root URL and *admin* to the correct pages (e.g., */ui/index.html*). These filters are commonly used in combination with the Amdatu Resource Handler.

Authentication

Authentication is implemented using Amdatu Security. There are two places where authentication applies: for customers to complete the ordering process and for the administrative backend in general.

The authentication check is implemented using a servlet filter. The filter uses the To kenProvider to read the token from the cookie in the request, validate it, and redirect the user to the login page if it's invalid or not set. The login page validates the user's credentials and then uses the TokenProvider to generate a new token, which is set in a cookie. Note that the login process and credential storage is an application-specific implementation. Different login mechanisms, for example, social logins, could be implemented on top of TokenProvider side by side.

Configuration Admin

The administration username and password can be configured in a configuration file. This is implemented using Configuration Admin in collaboration with Apache Felix File Install. File Install makes it easy to read configuration files from a directory and pass the configuration on to Configuration Admin. By default, Apache Felix File Install monitors a directory called *load*, hence the *load* directory in the run project.

The configuration is used by a Managed Service ConfigAdminLoginProvider. This service will become available when its configuration is available, and it will use the configured credentials to offer a login method.

Scheduled Jobs

A common requirement for real-world applications is to execute certain code at predetermined times (e.g., each night). In the example project, we use a schedule job to re-index the full text search index. Note that this is not necessarily the best way to work with a full text search index (a full re-index may be expensive), but it's a good example of a scheduled task.

The scheduling is based on Amdatu Scheduling. Amdatu Scheduling uses the white-board pattern to find services that implement the Job interface. The service should be annotated with parameters that declare the scheduling rules for the job, for example, that it runs every few hours or every night.

Event Admin

The search index is also updated each time a product is updated or removed. We use Event Admin to do this; the product service fires events (without knowing if there are any listeners) asynchronously, and another component acts as an event handler that re-indexes the updated product.

Testing

The example code shows that it is easy to achieve high test coverage using the technology stack discussed in this book. The project contains both unit and integration tests. Code that mostly depends on other services is unit tested, which is easy because service dependencies can be mocked easily. The unit tests are in the projects themselves.

The Mongo-based services are tested using Bnd integration tests; they run in an OSGi framework against a real MongoDB database. The integration tests are located in separate projects, postfixed with *.test*. The integration tests are based on a convenience base class from the Amdatu project. The base class has a convenient way to configure Managed Services and to declare service dependencies in the test.

Looking at one of the integration tests, we see a common pattern when using the Amdatu base class. The base class is generic and must be passed the interface of the service being tested in the constructor. The base class will then automatically make an instance of the service available in the `instance` variable after the setup method of the base class is invoked. The setup method of the base class will wait for a maximum of 10 seconds for service dependencies to become available.

Index

We'd like to hear your suggestions for improving our indexes. Send email to index@oreilly.com.

Apache Shindig, 126
Apache Wink, 114, 115
API bundles
    cloud application architecture, 96
    creating, 27
Application Servers, 167
architecture (see cloud application architecture)
Arquillian, 104, 105
artifacts column, 155
Aspect Oriented Programming (AOP), 4, 70–72
aspect services, 70–72
AspectJ, 70
Atlassian Clover, 78
authentication, 123
    (see also token-based security)
authorization (see token-based security)
AutoConf Resource Processor, 158
autoscaling, 159–164

B

BASE principles, 141
baselining, 47
Binary JSON (BSON), 143
BluePrint, 28
BND Maven plug-in, 12
Bndtools
    adding MetaType files to bundle, 62
    baselining versions, 47
    creating applications using, 26
    including static content in JAR, 109
    integration testing using, 48–49
    manifest imports, 19
    overview, 11
    project structure for cloud applications, 98–99
    repackaging JAR files, 79
    repositories in, 29
    specifying provider or consumer type, 47
    uses constraints, 21
BSON (Binary JSON), 143
Bundle-Activator class
    defined, 21
    registering service in, 30
Bundle-Name header, 18
Bundle-SymbolicName header, 18, 27
Bundle-Version header, 18
BundleContext, 43, 49, 72
bundles
    adding classes to, 30

API bundles, 96
benefits of using small, 95
cache for, 72–73
classloader, 81
cloud application architecture, 96
defined, 14
dependency for, 76–77
and Extender pattern, 65
format, 18
Fragment Bundles, 77
intra-bundle messaging, 68
manifest headers
    Bundle-Name, 18
    Bundle-SymbolicName, 18
    Bundle-Version, 18
    Export-Package, 20–21
    Import-Package, 19–20
    Require-Bundle, 20
passing bundle classloader manually, 81
shared resources in, 121
specifying in Run Requirements, 30
starting/stopping, 31
states of, 36
sub-bundles, 176
versions for, 48
viewing in Gogo, 31

C

cache, bundle, 72–73
callback methods
    during lifecycle, 42–43
    service registration and deregistration, 40
CDI (Context and Dependency Injection), 14
change, 3
classes
    adding to bundles, 30
    exporting, 14
    grouping of, 5
    internal, 7
    public, 13–14
classloading
    dynamic
        DynamicImport-Package, 87
        overview, 86–87
    problems with
        classpath scanning, 81
        overview, 80
        passing bundle classloader manually, 81
ClassNotFoundException, 19, 87, 132

S

X

X-Web-Resource-Version header, 113

X-WebResource header, 66, 67
XADataSource class, 133

About the Authors

Paul Bakker is a software architect for Luminis Technologies. His current focus is on building modular enterprise applications and the cloud. He believes that modularity and the cloud are the two main points we have to deal with to bring technology to the next level, and he is working on making this possible for mainstream software development. Today he is working on educational software focused on personalized learning for high school students in the Netherlands. He is also responsible for pushing technology forward. Luminis strongly believes in open source, and all the technology development they are doing happens in the open source community. Paul is an active contributor on projects such as Amdatu, Apache ACE, JBoss Forge, and BndTools. He has a background as trainer on Java-related technology and is a regular speaker at conferences.

Bert Ertman is a fellow at Luminis in the Netherlands. Next to his customer assignments, he is responsible for stimulating innovation, knowledge sharing, coaching, technology choices, and presales activities. Outside his day job, he is a Java User Group leader for NLJUG, the Dutch Java User Group. He is a frequent speaker on Enterprise Java and Software Architecture-related topics at international conferences (e.g., J-Fall, Devoxx, JavaOne, Jfokus, etc.) as well as an author and member of the editorial advisory board for Dutch software development magazine *Java Magazine*. In 2008, Bert was honored by being awarded the coveted title of Java Champion by an international panel of Java leaders and luminaries.

Colophon

The animal on the cover of *Building Modular Cloud Apps with OSGi* is a European Roller (*Coracias garrulus*).

The cover image is from *Meyers Kleines Lexicon*. The cover font is Adobe ITC Garamond. The text font is Adobe Minion Pro; the heading font is Adobe Myriad Condensed; and the code font is Dalton Maag's Ubuntu Mono.

Have it your way.

Get even more for your money.

Join the O'Reilly Community, and register the O'Reilly books you own. It's free, and you'll get:

- $4.99 ebook upgrade offer
- 40% upgrade offer on O'Reilly print books
- Membership discounts on books and events
- Free lifetime updates to ebooks and videos
- Multiple ebook formats, DRM FREE
- Participation in the O'Reilly community
- Newsletters
- Account management
- 100% Satisfaction Guarantee

Signing up is easy:

1. Go to: oreilly.com/go/register
2. Create an O'Reilly login.
3. Provide your address.
4. Register your books.

Note: English-language books only

To order books online:
oreilly.com/store

For questions about products or an order:
orders@oreilly.com

To sign up to get topic-specific email announcements and/or news about upcoming books, conferences, special offers, and new technologies:
elists@oreilly.com

For technical questions about book content:
booktech@oreilly.com

To submit new book proposals to our editors:
proposals@oreilly.com

O'Reilly books are available in multiple DRM-free ebook formats. For more information:
oreilly.com/ebooks

O'REILLY®

Spreading the knowledge of innovators   oreilly.com

Lightning Source UK Ltd.
Milton Keynes UK
UKHW051118201221
395970UK00006B/270